CONNECTIONS.

ROBERTSON, 1696-2010

A FAMILY HISTORY

By

LOARN D. ROBERTSON

Robertson, Loarn D. 1945-

Title: Connections. Robertson, 1696-2010 A Family History.

Includes descendants tree, surname derivations, clan affiliations, clan

mottos and kinship report.

ISBN: 13:978-1470094508

10:1470094509

Author: Loarn D. Robertson

Front Cover Illustration – An Atholl Highlander, c1900 (source J.R.R.E.)

DEDICATION

Jean Fernie.

Sui generis – the only one of (her) kind.

ACKNOWLEDGEMENTS

I am indebted to my sister Rosemary, my cousins Iona Legatt and June Robertson for their help in filling in many gaps in my knowledge, and providing materials to support the cause. I owe a lot to Alan Bowden who I was introduced to over the electronic airways. He helped lead me to a branch of the family I never knew existed. And, to the many long suffering librarians who patiently listened to my concerns and needs often making my interests their interests, invariably setting me to rights. I cannot forget Kathy Fuoss who helped piece the notes and scribbles together, and Joanne Brummett who brought the images to life. Thanks to *Alba Cartographics* for permission to use the map in Figure 2. Finally, I am most grateful to my wife Anne for her patience and encouragement in working with a professional procrastinator. To all of you a huge thanks

TABLE OF CONTENTS

PREFACE

On seeing the partially completed family tree of my Scottish ancestors that I was piecing together, my sister inquired, "Who are all these people?" In fact, I only knew a few names and then only limited information that connected them. At the time, I had also found a separate branch of the family that I never knew existed so the number of unknown names was mounting, and my sister's words resonated in my ears. I had started to develop a family tree for my own interest to see how far back I could trace the family name. My own children, now in the USA, had visited Scotland only a few times and still thought that the Scots talked "funny" and wore skirts. They certainly knew little or nothing about where family members had come from and what impact their lives had had on the family history or on society in general. For that matter, neither did I.

I decided that not only was a family tree required that showed names and dates, but also some sort of narrative about the life and times of our ancestors. Over the past several years, on a part time basis, I collected information from lots of different sources. Thank goodness for the Internet, for without that the story would indeed have been brief. Sites like *Scotland's People, Ancestry.com, Genuki.Fife*, the *LDS Family History Library, National Library of Scotland* and the *Clan Donnachaidh Society* have proved invaluable. When back in Scotland I was able to visit places like *Cupar Public Library, National Archives of Scotland*, (births, marriages, and deaths), together with the addresses of known family members. I combed through newspapers, directories, maps, wills, and a few letters. I took a few hiking expeditions tramping through graveyards and around streets and locals where ancestors once trod. I talked with those that knew a considerable amount about genealogical work and local histories. On one occasion, I was even interviewed, in Old Greyfriars Kirkyard, by students from Edinburgh University doing a video piece on why people like me are pottering about in churchyards.

You will see from the table of contents that I have listed chapters according to the known Robertson male line. Gender bias is intended! Each generation (G) is identified, and those Robertson males that marry and have issue have their Christian names underlined and are the subject(s) of the following chapter(s); while Robertson females that marry have their names italicized, and are considered within the same chapter. Complete family units are presented together. So, you may find that dates move forwards with successive generations of one family unit, then back to a previous, but older, family unit. Because there are so many names, and some that are repeated over the generations, you will find that somewhere within the narrative, I usually refer to a name with a birth date listed, parenthetically, immediately after. If you get lost, please refer to the *Descendants Tree* in chapter 1. That chapter has a full listing of all the names and the position of each person in the family tree, according to generation (G) shown before each name.

I have tried, where possible, to provide some record of the life of each ancestor, but sometimes little or nothing was known, or found, leaving gaps in the narrative. So, occasionally I have added an historical note, within each initial section entitled "Life and Times of….," to provide a brief backdrop to the story. For some readers, not so familiar with things Scottish, I have "translated" some terms and defined some others. There are occasional references to money. The old British system used pounds (L), shillings (s), and pennies (d) until 1970 when things went metric. To keep it simple I have rounded most values to pounds (L) and in a few cases have shown the relative worth today, also in pounds. Some may want to convert the relative worth to US dollars, by multiplying by about 2. A few commodities like meat and bread are listed and in some cases I present the retail relative worth of some of these items. In this I have to thank *Measuring Worth.com* for the use of their calculator. You may find a mixture of the Queen's English and word spellings found in a *Webster's New World Dictionary.* Being now transplanted in the USA has created a kind of schizophrenia in my ability to spell.

When reading, I think it would not hurt to have a map of Britain handy. I also found some old and some newer photos that I have included to help move the story along. At the end of the work you will also find four appendices that record some different aspects of the family history. The first appendix examines the several migrations of the family with specific locations and some addresses. The second appendix provides a list of surname derivations or clan affiliations for those with surnames, other than Robertson, that through marriage became part of the family. The third appendix lists occupations held by early family members. Finally, the fourth appendix is a kinship listing to the earliest known ancestor David Robertson together with some "Facts and Figures" about the family. The diversity and similarities within some of these appendices may surprise you.

I hope that if you read this work, you will find the narrative interesting and even amusing, in places. The read is aimed at trying to provide the story of our branch of the Robertson Clan together with the life and times of the family members. Maybe in the future, some devoted soul will choose to continue this work and develop it, or a branch of it, further. It can be most rewarding, such as meeting a cousin you never knew existed, finding a relative with a fascinating history, learning an historical family event that has import for today, or seeing parallels in looks, fashion consciousness, and behaviors across the generations. One thing is certain we are all connected.

LDR (Illinois, 2012).

CHAPTER 1

Descendants of David (Robbsone) Robertson.

1G David (Robbsone) Robertson 1690-
  + Suffia (Sophia) Deer 1689-
    2G Mary Robertson 1714-
    2G Isabel Robertson 1716-
    2G Elizabeth Robertson 1719-
    2G David Robertson 1722-
      +Isabel Jervies 1719/20-
      3G James Robertson 1753-
      3G Peter Robertson 1756-1816
        +Sophia Bell 1772-1816
        4G David Robertson 1796-
          +Anne Stewart 1799-
          5G Catherine Taylor Robertson 1828-
        4G James Robertson 1798-1856
          +Margaret Ireland 1807-1872
          5G Anne Robertson 1827-1876
          5G Sophia Robertson 1828-1831
          5G Peter Robertson 1831-1860
          5G Margaret Robertson 1833-1898
            +Robert Wallace 1831-1899
            6G Robert Lamb Wallace 1858-1894
            6G James Robertson Wallace 1860-
            6G William John Wallace 1861-1862
            6G Patrick Robertson Wallace 1862-
            6G Archibald Duncan Wallace 1864-
            6G Maggie Ireland Wallace 1866-
              +Alfred Gray
            6G Arthur Stanley Jowett Wallace 1872-
            6G Alfred Campbell Wallace 1875-1911
          5G Andrew Robertson 1836-1881
            +Janet Thallon 1838-1924
            6G Agnes Sophia Robertson 1866-
            6G Maggie Ireland Robertson 1867-1956
      {+ = Spouse}

+George Simpson 1860-1899
7G George Archibald Dundas Simpson 1892-
6G Annie Hay Robertson 1869-
+Charles Wood 1874-1953
7G A. Thallon Wood
6G James Robertson 1872-
5G James Robertson 1839-1907
+Margaret Elizabeth McVeagh 1847-1906
6G Patrick James Robertson 1872-1961
+Mabel Wilhelmina Despard 1872-1926
7G Douglas Robertson 1904-1977
+Laura Elizabeth Talbot-Smith 1912-1994
8G Loarn Despard Robertson 1945-
+Anne Marlene Scott 1956-
9G Rory Duncan Robertson 1979-
9G Rachael Despard Robertson 1982-
9G Keegan Jean Robertson 1985-
+ Anthony D. Aggers 1983-
10G Felicity Anne Aggers 2010-
9G Mairi Alexandra Robertson 1989-
8G Rosemary Struan Robertson 1951-
+ Landale Cranfield 1952-
9G Laura Cranfield (adopted) 1988-
*2nd Husband of Rosemary Struan Robertson:
+Peter Lawry 1945 -
7G Aileen Robertson 1910-1984
7G Marion Hazel Robertson 1915-1919
6G Jessie Eva Robertson 1873-1949
+Hugh Wallace Aitken 1865-1947
7G Wallace Aitken 1904-1971
+Eilla Mabel Laird 1905-1992
8G Iona Laird Aitken 1947-
+John Brian Leggat 1948-
9G James Douglas Leggat 1982-
9G Joanna Rachel Leggat 1983-
8G Garry Robertson Aitken 1949-
+Jane Anne Finlayson Strathdee 1950
9G Steven Damian Aitken 1975-

*2nd Wife of Garry Robertson Aitken:
+Margaret Anne McGregor 1947 -
9G Scott Gregor Aitken 1984-
9G Ross Garry Aitken 1985-
7G Kenneth Aitken 1905-1944
7G Malcolm Aitken 1907-1999
+Margorie Winifred Judd 1905 - 2006
8G Ian Malcolm Aitken 1936-
+Hazel Faith Lock 1942-
9G Mairi Elaine Zoe Aitken 1964-1964
9G Kenneth Malcolm Harold Aitken 1965-
9G Fergus Shaun Wallace Aitken 1967-
+Fiona Elizabeth McCallum 1969-
10G Sophie Gemma Aitken 1999-
10G Finlay James Lewis Aitken 2001-
9G Tristan Francis Ian Aitken 1971-
+Elizabeth Gallagher 1964-
10G Philip Ruiriadh Braden Aitken 1996-
10G Chloe Brianna Amber Aitken 1998-
8G Hamish Wilsoun Aitken 1939-
+Carolyn Betty Allen 1943-
9G Douglas Wilsoun Aitken 1972-
9G Robert Malcom Aitken 1974-
+Virginie Durlot 1978 -
7G Douglas Aitken 1911-1935
6G Elsie Robertson 1875-1954
+William Arrol 1839-1913
*2nd Husband of Elsie Robertson:
+Robert John Collie 1860-1935
6G Maud Robertson 1878-1944
6G Ronald Douglas Robertson 1883-1968
+Mary (Molly) Wills 1889-1963
7G Margaret Elizabeth Pearce Robertson 1918-1992
7G James Pearce Robertson 1920-2000
+June O'Carroll Scott 1928-
5G David Robertson 1841-1868
3G Janet Robertson 1758-
3G Margaret Robertson 1760-

CHAPTER 2

Origins

A few years ago, I attended my sister's wedding on the Isle of Skye. After a very festive time, I managed a few days pottering about the island, and was able to visit a former teacher, from my schooldays at the Glasgow Academy, Colonel Lachlan (Lachie) Robertson.

Lachie had retired to Elgol, on the far eastern side of the island. It was a feat just to get there. A one track, switchback road, with sheep and cattle meandering about; blind hilltops, and errant vehicles on the road that forced you to back up, and find a pull-off to let them by. Elgol, of course, is a romantic spot for many Scots. It was here in 1746, as Lachie described it, that Prince Charles Edward Stewart (Bonnie Prince Charlie), the last of the Royal Stewarts to claim the throne, scampered across the hillsides being pursued by Redcoat troops, after the battle of Culloden. He had raised the Clans, about a year earlier, in a fateful attempt to retake the British crown from the Hanovarians. He hid, for a time, in the caves below Elgol, and was later whisked away by the heroine Flora MacDonald to Portree where he boarded a fishing vessel and escaped the English naval blockade and landed safely in France, never to return.

Lachie had been a most esteemed geography master, at the Academy, and he was no slouch at coaching rugby football, having many successful boys' teams and at least one Scottish International that passed through his capable hands. It seemed, to me, a fitting place and time to ask a fellow Robertson about the clan. Lachie was adamant that we (Robertson's) all hailed from central Scotland around Rannoch Moor and the Glen Garry in what is now Perth & Kinross. His branch of Clan Robertson had migrated to Skye many generations ago, and successive generations had lived in Skye, ever since. My father, Douglas (1903), went one better. He asserted that his branch had been a part of the Struan Robertson's, the family from which all the chiefs of the clan are descended. My sister's middle name was also Struan, and that, to my mind made the bond complete. After all, who would deny their aristocratic background?

Figure 1. Colonel Lachlan & Mrs. Robertson, Elgol, Isle of Skye (2004). Pointing out the escape route of Bonnie Prince Charlie.

When I started to look backward, in time, for my ancestors, I always thought that I would eventually find a name geographically positioned somewhere near Rannoch Moor, in the heart of Robertson territory. But, that was not to be. At least it has not been up to this point. Certainly, the paper trail of names seemed to be heading in that direction, but ended abruptly in Fife. I was unable to find any relevant name farther north. Somewhat in desperation I decided to try the evolving technology of genetic blood line "fingerprinting" using my DNA, extracted from "y" chromosomes, to try and link with another Robertson's DNA in the old ancestral hunting grounds in Perthshire. So far, there have been 50-60 matches with my DNA, but most of these are weak links with no clear surname association. Two names, from DNA testing, one Reid and another Reed (different spelling) showed a stronger association with my DNA, but these names do not appear in the family tree. It may surprise you to learn that more than 350 persons with a Robertson surname are currently part of a clan genetics project. Most of these folks, as you might suspect, are abroad and are trying to find a connection back to "the old country," and some have been successful.

However, our branch of the Robertson clan has no worry about the connection to Scotland, for it is established. The oldest ancestor that I found was David Robertson (or Robbsone) who was in Fife in the early 1700s. The surname "Robbsone" is one of the many spelling variants that emerged when consulting old documents. Other variations, that were found, have been corrected.

DAVID (ROBBSONE) ROBERTSON (1G), was born about 1690. He married SUFFIA (SOPHIA) DEER May 25, 1711 in Newburn, Fife, daughter of ALEXANDER DEER and JAIN HARVEY. She was born 1689 in Newburn, Fife.
David and Sophia had four children MARY born 1714, ISABEL born 1716, ELIZABETH born 1719, and DAVID born 1722. David was to carry the Robertson name forwards

LIFE AND TIMES OF DAVID (ROBBSONE) ROBERTSON:
It is unknown where David was born, but his birth likely coincided with "The Glorious Revolution," when the hereditary line of Royal Stewarts, whose family had provided a succession of Kings and Queens, lost power and was replaced by the Dutch King William and his British born Queen Mary. There were many reasons for this but at the heart of the matter was the catholic religion of the then Stewart King James 11, and his inability to read the mood of his subjects. In 1688 there was rebellion in Scotland against the new protestant King William. In Clan Robertson territory, at a place called Killiecrankie, just off the present A9 road, a force of Jacobites (followers of James) routed a government army. The government army later reformed with Cameronian reserves and a further pitched battle took place on the streets of Dunkeld, on the southern tip of Robertson Clan lands on the River Tay. With hand to hand fighting in

15

the streets, the town was all but destroyed, before the Jacobites, suffering from a lack of support, withdrew to their clan lands.

For the next forty years trouble continued to brew. It should be remembered that Scotland, at this time, was a dreadfully poor country, with a gross national product about $1/40^{th}$ that of England. Only a few

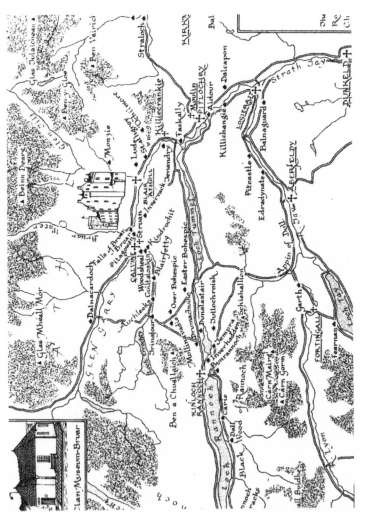

Figure 2. Illustration of old Clan Robertson territory in Perth & Kinross Showing Dunkeld, Killiecrankie, Struan, Loch Rannoch and other places.

landowners had any power and they wanted more. The only way to achieve that, they thought, was a union with England which was ratified in 1707. When that happened, many believed that Scotland had lost her independence as well as her Parliament. A few "elected" officials in Westminster, London, now represented Scottish interests.

The reality was that only personal interests were usually served. The Union also heralded the Hanoverian (German) succession to the throne and a requirement of a protestant faith for the incumbent. Many in Scotland opposed this Union and further rebellions occurred. Feelings against the Union ran so high in old clan Robertson territory that 4000 Highlanders were raised to march against the government of the day. This was probably the largest gathering or armed Highlanders ever raised on former Robertson lands, and with difficulty they were eventually convinced to stand down.

In 1709 a Jacobite force reinforced with French troops, anchored off the Isle of May, near the Fife coast, hoping to land at Burntisland and gather reinforcements. Bad weather and an English naval squadron forced the rebels to retire. When the first Hanoverian monarch arrived in 1715 another Jacobite rebellion arose. This time a land force of Jacobites met a government army at a place called Sherrifmuir, about 39 miles due west of the parish of Newburn in Fife. About 300 were killed on both sides, and no clear victor could be determined. Again, the Jacobites, lacking support melted away back to their glens.

Newburn lies between the A 917 - the Upper Largo to Elie road, and the A 915 -Upper Largo to St. Andrews road. The parishes of Largo and Kilconquhar act as bookends to Newburn. The evidence suggests that it is here that our branch of the Robertson clan was to be found in the late 17th century and family members were there until the late 1700s.

The name of David Robertson appears on his marriage certificate to Sophia Deer (or Dire) in the parish of Newburn, in 1711. David's name also appears as a subtenant in the village of Moorhead in 1722.

Moorhead no longer exists but the name can be found in the *Ordnance Survey Maps* of Fife around 1745. The village was located north of Newburn Kirk and about midway between the prominent mounds of Largo Law and Lonehead. All of David's four children Mary, Isabel, Elizabeth and David were born in Newburn. Nothing could be found on David's three sisters, but he carried the Robertson name forwards.

Figure 3. Map of Newburn Parish, Fife showing Moorhead, between Largo Law and Lonehead (top). Newburn Kirk is to the right and Lower Largo to the left. (c 1790).

CHAPTER 3

DAVID ROBERTSON (2G) was born May 27, 1722 in Newburn, Fife. He married ISABEL JERVIES July 15, 1742 in Elie, Fife. She was the daughter of DAVID JERVEES and ISOBEL TAILZIOUR. She was born March 20, 1719/20 in Elie, Fife.

David and Isabel had four children JAMES born 1753, <u>PETER</u> born 1756, JANET born 1760, and MARGARET born 1760. Peter was to carry the family name forwards.

LIFE AND TIMES OF DAVID ROBERTSON:

When David was born in 1722 there was a severe food shortage in Fife and other Scottish counties. A new tax system and the appearance of aggressive customs men, along the coast, prompted riots. At Pittenweem, a small harbor village in Fife about six miles from Moorhead, a certain Andrew Wilson and George Robertson , beat up a customs official and robbed him. They were caught, tried and condemned to hang in Edinburgh. But, during a moment when the guards were distracted, Robertson escaped, never to be heard of again. The unfortunate Wilson was left to swing, but an angry mob gathered and in turn lynched the officer in charge of the hanging. Disturbances like these created additional unrest along the Fife coast and in other Scottish towns.

The government was concerned that more problems would erupt in the Highlands and wanted a way to check and pacify that area. The English General Wade, nicknamed "The Road Builder" was sent to do the job. Besides, building new forts, refurbishing older ones, and collecting illegal arms, he was best known for building about 40 bridges and four roadways through the Highlands. The idea was to speedily move government troops to trouble spots. Many of these constructions still exist today, including the magnificent five arched bridge across the River Tay at Dunkeld, on the edge of Robertson lands. There is also a smaller bridge at Struan village where many of the Robertson Chiefs used to live. One of the major roads built by General Wade, goes North over the pass at Killiecrankie to Inverness. This same road probably brought more commerce to Perth in the south, and to points east in the county of Fife.

Figure 4. Anne Robertson & local artist and historian Roger Lee – Old Struan Kirkyard (2004). A Wade built bridge is in the background.

David and his family lived through the upheavals of the last of the Jacobite rebellions aimed at retaking the British crown for the Stewarts. The leader was Prince Charles Edward Stewart, grandson of the James 11 who had lost the throne earlier in 1689. The same roads so carefully constructed for transporting government troops, by General Wade, now carried the Highland rebels southward in 1745. A year later, the roads were again used to move the Jacobite army north, but this time in full retreat. The Jacobites were eventually routed at

Culloden, outside Inverness. It marked the final defeat of the Celts at the hands of the Anglo-Saxons. This was a dangerous time in Scotland and the brutality that followed Culloden, the occupation of Scottish lands by government troops, and the "Clearances" of people and property in the north, created, in some, great animosity against the government, south of the border.

The uncertainties of life at this time may have been instrumental in delaying David and Isabel from having children. Fife, being a peninsula, may have shielded our ancestors from some of the fallout from the Jacobite rebellions, but there is no doubt that they would have felt the reverberations. David was 30 when his first child, James, arrived. In 1756, David was listed as a tenant in Craighead, just north of where Moorehead once stood. He, like his father probably worked the land, but he had friends that were weavers (John Johnston and Thomas White—witnesses to the birth of his children) in "Balbaird" and he was likely associating with more skilled workers that may have influenced his ambitions with regard to his children's future.

Today, there are only a few homes scattered around Newburn Parish with a rough, single lane road meandering through it. There are few records describing the area, but in the *Statistical Accounts of Scotland* in 1795, Reverend Lawrie provides some interesting observations. He indicated that the Parish was blessed with very fertile soil that produced wheat, potatoes, and luxuriant turnip crops. Newburn was a pretty area with woods, waters, hills, and dales. At the time of the writing of the account there were about "456 souls" but by the end of the 1880s that number had dwindled to 344. In 1794 there were only seven "poor persons" in the parish who were supported by Sunday collections, but retained their own homes and were supplied according to need. The minister also noted that the parish harbored many "seceders" (from the true Kirk) including Cameronians, Independents, the Burugh Congregation, and the Relief Congregation—about 32 souls. He notes greater tolerance for these "seceders," than in times past and that the people in general were "sober, regular, and industrious." He was also pleased to report that several elders of the Relief Congregation had returned to the Established Church. The parochial school had "considerable repute" and offered English, writing, arithmetic, and Latin for a few shillings for those that can pay. Scholars, who were poor could attend the grammar school in "Drumelry" (old name for Newburn) courtesy of a benefactor, John Wood of Orkie.

Figure 5. Ruin of the Established Church at Newburn. View from the south (2004).

A farm workers wage was seven pounds sterling for men, and three pounds for women, per annum. A mason could get up to two shillings per day (relative worth today is about 7.9 pounds) and a tailor up to one shilling. Beef, veal and mutton cost 3.5 pennies per pound (relative worth today is about 1.16 pounds). The minister was also concerned about the weight of the bread that he felt should be regulated as some bakers were undercutting their customers.

The old ruined Kirk in Newburn was about 55 feet long but only just over 12 feet wide. A new Kirk was built about a mile to the west of the old one. In "Balchristie," on the east side of the parish, about a mile due east of Drumelry there lies a foundation of a very old church that belonged to the "Culdees," those ascetic monks who spread the

Columban ministry, from Iona, during the 9/10th centuries. The minister goes on to suggest that the church was one of the first Christian churches in Scotland, the monks having landed on the inviting sands of Largo Bay. That is probably a stretch of the truth, but the view from the old Kirk is certainly inviting with gentle grasslands and cultivated fields, sweeping southward toward the sands of Largo Bay.

All of David's four children were born in Newburn, but only Peter, the second child could be traced and he carried the Robertson name forwards. However, the names of James, Janet and Margaret appear later as Christian names among other family members.

Figure 6.Looking through the south portal of Newburn Church. Robertson family members & Largo Bay beyond (2004).

CHAPTER 4

PETER ROBERTSON (3G), was born May 17, 1756 in
Newburn, Fife and died July 26, 1816 in Cupar, Fife. He married
SOPHIA BELL May 22, 1791 in Cupar, Fife, Scotland, daughter of
JOHN BELL and ANNA STENHOUSE. She was born April 26,
1772 in Aberdour, Fife, and died May 1816 in Cupar, Fife.

Peter and Sophia had two children DAVID born 1796, and
<u>JAMES</u> born 1798. James was to carry the family name forwards.

LIFE AND TIMES OF PETER ROBERTSON:

Peter was born during the hey day of the Scottish Enlightenment,
when for about 60 years there was a great outpouring of intellectual
activity in Scotland. Men of genius like Robert Adam (architect),
David Hume (philosopher), Henry Raeburn (painter), Adam Smith
(economist) and William Robertson (historian), contributed to the
intellectual life of the nation. They and others were progressives and
Unionists (union with England) and during their tenure, Scottish cities
like Glasgow grew with its expanding port supporting new trade
commodities like tobacco. The men of the Enlightenment had no
truck with the "medieval" activities of the Jacobites.

During this time, too, Peter prospered although when and how he
acquired the skills of a flesher is unknown. Sometime before 1790 he
decided to strike out on his own and moved from Newburn to the
bustling market town of Cupar, about eight miles to the north. He set
up shop as a butcher, somewhere in Cupar, and then met and married
Sophia Bell. She probably moved from Aberdour, a small fishing
village on the Firth of Forth, with her parents at about the same time
as Peter moved to Cupar.

Peter also may have been aware of rebellion in the air with the
American War of Independence and growing hostilities with the
French. His new business may well have benefited from the effects of
war in providing meat for hungry soldiers in training at home and
fighting overseas.

When Peter arrived in Cupar it was growing quickly and was to be the county seat until the 1990s. The older part of town lay on the north side of the River Eden and to the south of the small river known as Lady Burn. The town's name may have come from the Gaelic "Comhpairt," meaning common land or pasture. The town became a royal burgh in David IIs time in the 12th century. There was a royal castle in Cupar in the 13th century, and was visited by Edward 1st of England ("Long Shanks"). Nothing remains of the castle, today. Moot Hill, on the western side of the town, might have been a defensive place or even a place where laws were enacted. At the start of the 19th century the population in Cupar may have been around 5,000, more than ten times the size of the parish of Newburn.

The town center is built around two main streets, Bonnygate and Crossgate. The administrative parts of the town, the Townhouse and County buildings were situated near the junction of these two roads. The streets were paved making transportation easier. A new parish church had been built in the 15th century on the Kirkgate near the town center, but there were other places of worship including a Free Church, Baptist, Episcopalian Chapel and at least one other Presbyterian church. There seemed to be little rancor between those holding slightly different religious beliefs and people were civil to one another. The homes were generally in good shape and the only blight was the "Iron House" or town jail that lay on the south side of the River Eden. As an accommodation it was described as "filthy and wretched." It was wanting for light, was dank, and forbidding and in an age of enlightenment was a disgrace to the town.

Apparently, there were a few impediments to greater industry within the town and these included contentious burgh politics and idleness and vice that accompanied the burugh politics. Also, too many tradesmen were frequenting the numerous taverns and losing much of their profits to drink. At this time there were 43 licensed alehouses in Cupar (that's about one alehouse per 93 people). Cupar had another disadvantage, that of having no seaport which meant increasing costs moving materials to and from Cupar. A suggestion was made in the early 19th century to create a navigable canal from the Eden to the sea. Textile mills were growing around the Eden, and

Cupar was becoming a county storehouse for iron, tar, ropes, bricks, tile wines, spirits, feeds, soap, candles, tobacco, tea, sugar, fruit, and all kinds of groceries.

As in Newburn the "Poor Rates" helped support those in need. In 1800 about 15 families received weekly support from the Kirk sessions. There were also the beginnings of pension funds where societies of tradesmen gave in support of indigent workers and the aging. But, the growing wealth of Cupar was attracting beggars who were traveling north and south of the town. On the site of the old Grammar School on Castle Hill, Madras Academy was founded in 1831. The Town Council regulated fees for Latin, English, writing, and arithmetic, from 1 shilling and 6 pence to 3 shillings for each quarter. Other subjects were taught, also, and the school enjoyed a high reputation.

The town was noted for its clean air, running water, and rolling hills that were thought to aid the health of the community. Small pox was better controlled and people were living longer, with some over 100 years of age. Only one natural phenomenon was to be feared and that was thunderstorms. Lightening from these storms accounted for the early demise of several town residents.

The introduction of the potato in the latter part of the 18th century to Cupar really helped laborers and their families to sustain themselves with this new food. Other foods were becoming more expensive—butter 9d/lb, cheese 5d/lb, eggs 4d per dozen, and salmon 5d/lb. The Robertsons were able to get 4d/lb for their meat products compared to 1.5d/lb for the generation before. However, the Robertsons also had competition because they were one of 16 flesher businesses that were operating in Cupar in the early 1800s. Of the 33 different occupations listed in Cupar, only eight contained larger numbers of professionals than fleshers, including wrights, tailors, and shoemakers.

But, life in Cupar also offered a fairly varied social life with, a horticultural society, a philharmonic society, as well as curling, cricket, and other games. Peter was to take an active life in the community and became a prominent member of the Fleshers Guild and was at one time a Deacon.

DAVID ROBERTSON, Peter's first son, was born June 19, 1796 in Cupar, Fife. He married ANNE STEWART December 21, 1823 in Cupar, Fife. She was born February 28, 1799 in Cupar, Fife.

Little could be found about David and his wife Anne, but it is likely they both moved out of Cupar to Little Dunkeld on the southern border of old clan Robertson territory. The fleshing business was left to his younger brother James. David and Anne had one child CATHERINE TAYLOR ROBERTSON, born October 17, 1828, in Little Dunkeld, Perthshire. Her Christian name is not among the other Robertson family names or known relative names.

CHAPTER 5

JAMES ROBERTSON (4G) was born March 7, 1798 in Cupar, Fife and died December 14, 1856 in Cupar. He married MARGARET IRELAND June 28, 1826 in Cupar, daughter of ANDREW IRELAND. She was born 1807 in Kilconquhar, Fife, and died October 10, 1872 at 21 Bonnygate, Cupar, Fife.

James and Margaret had seven children ANNE born in 1827, SOPHIA born 1828, PETER born 1831, *MARGARET* born 1833, ANDREW born 1836, JAMES born 1839, and DAVID born in 1841. Andrew and James carried the Robertson name forwards.

LIFE AND TIMES OF JAMES ROBERTSON:

James was born at a time of continuing unrest due to hostilities with France. The French, like the Americans, had their own revolution and overthrew the establishment, but unlike the American Revolution, the French, unfortunately, paved the way for another imperialist leader, in the form of Napoleon Bonaparte.

Again, the fleshing business probably prospered through government contracts for beef and mutton for the troops. But, in 1815, at the conclusion of the Napoleonic wars, Scotland suffered from a severe depression, and many Scots were bitter in seeing their families suffer after years of faithful service against the French.

Political radicalism emerged, fueled by both the American and French revolutions that railed against the constitution that protected and supported the privileges of the landowners and the merchants. Strikes erupted in Scotland and some radicals were killed in clashes with militia. Some were imprisoned and others were transported. The Whig (forerunners to the modern day liberals) minority in Scotland, numbering only about 4000 saw that the only way to avert revolution was in parliamentary reform through an extension of the franchise. James joined this populist movement and became politically involved in Cupar.

In 1832, the year after James's son Peter was born in Cupar, a Whig government pushed through the Reform Act that signaled the end of the old ways in Scotland, in which a few hundred landowners controlled the destiny of the nation. James began to take an active interest in the running of the town of Cupar both from his position as a merchant and as a citizen. His father had been Dean of the Guild and in 1833 James was elected a Councilor and also as Dean of the Guild. His political leanings lay with the Whigs (liberals), but Tories (conservatives) and some radicals were also to be found in Cupar. The local newspaper, the *Fifeshire Journal*, seemed to have strong conservative leanings, but reported on what were a number of contentious elections. In this election one writer said that "I would have liked to see more conservatives in the Council, yet we cannot withhold our admiration of the unbending integrity and sterling talent of the radical portion of it, and we look upon that party (the Whigs) with all their faults as a wholesome ingredient in the Council.

In 1838 James was a Liberal candidate for Cupar municipal elections against the Tories. The feelings ran strong in both parties. An Editorial note condemned the Whigs for attempting to ostracize Tory candidates when the community feeling was against Whig politicians. The editorial continued "the unsuccessful party (Whigs) were sanguine over the earlier part of the forenoon, but saw, about 12 o'clock, we believe, that the day was against them."

In 1841 James was again back in politics and was asked to stand against a conservative J.M. Graham, a surgeon. A letter he wrote to the *Fifeshire Journal* ran as follows—"Gentlemen, having received a Requisition, subscribed by a numerous and respectable portion of the Guildry, requesting me to stand as a Candidate for the Office of Dean of Guild at the ensuing election. I feel it my duty to comply . . ."

James's nomination raised the ire of the Journal Editor who wrote "the movements of our local Whigs, like those of a certain animal, are only made known by the little dirty heaps they throw up in their progress." So began the Editorial essentially condemning the Whigs for nominating James for the Deanship of the Guild against Dr. Graham. The Editorial continues "both men are honest citizens, affable neighbors, and men of good understanding. Both are equally qualified to discharge the burghal or commercial part of their duty, but further than this there is no comparison." On the basis of Dr. Graham's past educational support, in Cupar, and some ability in securing of money to assist the poor to get an education, he was perceived to be the better candidate. The Editorial conceded that "we do not accuse Mr. Robertson of hostility to the cause of education— his interest as a parent is sufficiently strong to prevent that, at least." The Editorial accused James of having been used by the Whigs as "they see in him the worthy and inoffensive citizen, and calculating on support for him on personal attachment, they have brought him forward as the only man they had a chance to carry."

At the election, many Guild brothers from towns like Dundee, Leith, Edinburgh, and other places, arrived for the vote. James was further castigated as "lending himself to a faction who have all clung, for the sheerest political and personal motives, positively obstructed the cause and spread of education in Cupar." James was elected by a majority of 686 to 58. "A result much to be regretted," ran the editorial in the *Fifeshire Journal*. The editorial concluded "we will keep watch on him (James Robertson) and see if he will really perform that act of mercy to these poor ignorant children who have been thrust out from the means of education."

There is no mention of how James performed, but he continued to be elected for Council positions through 1845 and beyond. In 1845 James also received a government contract to deliver pork. Not wanting to miss an opportunity he took out a notice in the *Fifeshire Journal* which read "Having been appointed Agent for Fife and the adjoining counties for executing a Government contract for the supply of PORK, hereby intimates that he is ready to give the highest price for pigs to be delivered either at Cupar or Dundee, of good quality (weight not an object if otherwise suitable). N.B. James Robertson will be glad to receive offers for Agencies in the counties of Fife, Kinross, Clackmannan, Stirling, and Perth, to whom commission will be allowed."

In the *1851 census*, James was listed as the head of the house at 21 Bonnygate. His wife Margaret and children Anne, Margaret, Andrew, James, and David were all listed. Peter, his eldest son, was not listed.

In addition James's father-in-law Andrew Ireland, was living there and he was born in Ceres, Fife. Two others were in the house. Agnes Speco, a house servant (18 years) and James Ritchie (17 years) a servant and apprentice Flesher. A total of 10 persons were in the house on census night. In addition, James employed two men to help with the business.

Figure 7. Family members outside 19 Bonnygate, Cupar, Fife. (2004). Location of the former Robertson Flesher shop.

When James died in 1856 he had an assessment of about 4,819 pounds sterling (relative worth today is about 3.5 million pounds) which included 748 pounds sterling in debts and 87 pounds sterling in household inventory. He held accounts with Scottish Equitable Insurance, Scottish Provident, Commercial Bank of Cupar, British Linen Company in Cupar, Clydesdale Bank, City of Glasgow, Western Bank of Scotland (more than 2000 pounds sterling) and shares in Cupar Gas Company. Although the buildings were not valued the house included a parlor, dinning room, lobby, two bedrooms, a garret with two bedsteads, kitchen with some bedding, a wash house, a shop (containing beams, scales, weights, knives, china, crystal), which may have been attached to the house. James also owned two fat cattle and six sheep. All his children had survived him (Peter, Andrew, James, David, Anne, and Margaret) and Margaret, his wife, was named executor of his will.

MARGARET IRELAND ROBERTSON, James's wife, must have been a good manager as she took over running the family business with her daughter Anne and son Andrew.

In 1861 Margaret and all her children were living at 21 Bonnygate, but by 1871 she and Anne were living at 19 Bonnygate. Agnes Laing, a widow, who was a hired help and Hellen Stoddart who was listed as an unmarried servant were also living there. Number 19 may have been the flesher shop in 1871, although today it is a barbershop. The location of the shop is ideal as it lies on the north side of Bonnygate where the road narrows as it approaches the market square at the junction of Bonnygate and Millgate roads. Lady Wynd bound the shop and house, on one side and what is now Balmarino Place, on the other. The nearness of the market-square and the funneling of traffic through the east end of Bonnygate must have delivered a large clientele for the shop.

When Margaret died in 1872 the assessment made was for 4731 pounds sterling (relative worth today is about 3.4 million pounds) . This included effects of the house and shop totaling 152 pounds sterling. The family had accounts, although small, with National Bank of Scotland, City of Glasgow Bank, Royal Bank of Scotland, British Linen Company Bank, Heritable Securities Investment Association

Ltd Edinburgh (over 1000 pounds sterling), Scottish Equitable Life Assurance Co. (358 pounds sterling). About 16 local customers owed money to Margaret, and it also looks like a renter had been taken in as some rent was due.

The listed surviving children were Anne, Margaret, Andrew, and James. Margaret was also identified as the wife of Robert Wallace, Minister of Old Greyfriars Church in Edinburgh. The children were all named as executors of the estate and they were instructed to pay off funeral expenses, debts, and legacies. Anne was the first concern. If she was unmarried, at Margaret's death, then she was to receive the furniture and plenishings (shop equipment) together with the proceeds of insurance policies and bonuses from the Scottish Equitable Assurance Co. If she was childless the estate was to be divided equally among lawful issue and if no issue then divided among survivors. Otherwise, the estate was to be divided among heirs and survivors. Anne never married.

ANNE ROBERTSON, James's first child, was born April 15, 1827, Cupar, and died February 9, 1876 in Cupar.
In the *1851 Census* Anne was listed as being 23 years old and living at 21 Bonnygate. In her mother's will she was listed as executor and was probably living at 75 Bonnygate in Cupar when her mother died in 1872. The move was probably to allow her brother Andrew and his family to occupy the premises. She was likely very involved with running the family business with her brother Andrew, after the death of her mother.

At time of her death, Anne's estate was worth 3,250 pounds sterling (relative worth today is about 2.3 million pounds) - a considerable amount for a single woman at the time. The estate included all the household furniture and silver plate. In addition, there were deposits in the Oriental Bank, the National Bank of Scotland, the National Mercantile Bank of India/London, and two security bonds in the Central Register of Sasines (July 1870 and July 1873).

One third of the estate was left to Margaret (Robertson) Wallace in life rent. One third of the estate went to Andrew Robertson in life rent and to his children. One third of the estate went to James Robertson and his heirs to be paid to him on first term of Whitsunday or Martinmas after her death.

Individual requests were as follows:

1. House furnishings to be divided up among three families (the Wallaces, Andrew Robertsons, and the James Robertsons). Mahogany Drawers owned by Margaret Ireland to be kept in family. The Honiton lace was to be divided between Margaret McVeagh (James's wife) and Janet Thallon Robertson (Andrew's wife). White petticoats were to be divided among the nieces together with the napery (household table linen).

2. Andrew Robertson—two dozen napkins, all electroplated articles except largest oval salver, six solid silver ladles, and the best dinner set. The Albert brooch went to Janet Robertson.

3. Sophia (niece), James (nephew), and Janet Robertson—dinner table, solid silver vas, divider, gravy spoons, 18 table spoons, 12 desert spoons, 2/4 salt spoons, electroplated oval salver. For Sophia, there was an old watch and another Albert brooch. A bracelet and locket containing locks of Sophia's hair and Anne's hair .

4. Margaret Wallace—12 large solid tea spoons and tongs, eye glass and mourning broach with Peter's hair, small forget-me-not pearl ring and bouquet holder, clothing pieces as she wants and then divide clothing among others, as she wants.

5. Margaret McVeagh—Margaret Ireland's large pebble brooch and finest filled plaid.

6. Maggie Ireland (niece)—small gold brooch with pebble fruit knife and vinegiretto.

7. Annie Hay (niece)—Emerald brooch, gold bracelet and earrings, worktable.

8. Jessie Eva (niece)—blue ring.

9. Elsie (niece)—pearl brooch.

SOPHIA ROBERTSON, James's second child, was born May 15, 1828, Cupar, Fife and died April 27, 1831, in Cupar.

Sophia was three when she died. She contracted measles that often proved fatal for youngsters in those days.

PETER ROBERTSON, James's third child was born February 25, 1831, in Cupar, Fife, and died June 6, 1860, in Cupar, Fife.

Peter, as the eldest son, did not follow father into the family business but became a Customs Officer in London. What is know is that he returned to Cupar, probably because he was ill with tuberculosis and stayed at 21 Bonnygate where he was cared for by his mother and sister Anne.

A helpful feature of the death certificates of the 1860s was that the final resting-place was sometimes indicated. In Peter's case he was listed as having been buried in the Cupar Churchyard, of the established Church. Most of the other Robertson's living in Cupar are likely to have been buried there too, but no monument remains to their memory. A few family members became rebels and joined the Presbyterian Free Church and became "wee Frees" as my father was fond of calling them.

Peter's personal estate, at time of death, was valued at 566 pounds sterling. This included a small amount of outstanding salary (five pounds), Policy of Assurance on Life (536 pounds), and body clothes, gold watch and chain (25 pounds).

His mother Margaret (Ireland) Robertson was named as executor and was bequeathed all his "worldly goods."

Specific requests included:

1. 100 pounds to Anne Robertson for her "kindness and attention" during Peter's last illness.

2. 50 pounds went to Margaret (Robertson) Wallace wife of Reverend William Wallace, Newton on Ayr.

3. 20 pounds sterling went to a friend (William Pitcairn) at 27 Church Road, Kingsland, London.

MARGARET ROBERTSON, James's fourth child, was born October 21, 1833 in Cupar, Fife, and died 1898 in London, England. She married ROBERT WALLACE March 12, 1858 in Cupar, Fife, Scotland, son of JASPER WALLACE and ELIZABETH ARCHIBALD. He was born June 24, 1831 in Ceres, Fife, and died June 6, 1899 in Westminster Hospital, London.

Margaret and Robert had eight children. ROBERT LAMB WALLACE was born December 12, 1858, Newton on Ayr, Ayr, and died in 1894 in London.

JAMES ROBERTSON WALLACE was born March 23, 1860, Newton on Ayr. According to the *1891 census* he was studying medicine in Edinburgh, and his residence at the time was 50 George Street, Edinburgh.

WILLIAM JOHN WALLACE was born October 31, 1861 in Edinburgh Parish, Edinburgh, Midlothian, and died in 1862.

PATRICK ROBERTSON WALLACE, was born October 25, 1862 in Edinburgh Parish, Edinburgh, Midlothian. In 1881 he was living with his brother James at 50 George Street in Edinburgh.

ARCHIBALD DUNCAN WALLACE was born April 3, 1864 in Edinburgh parish, Edinburgh, Midlothian.

MAGGIE IRELAND WALLACE, was born August 27, 1866 in Edinburgh parish, Edinburgh, Midlothian. She would later marry ALFRED GRAY in London.

ARTHUR STANLEY JOWETT WALLACE, was born February 8, 1872 in Edinburgh, Midlothian.

ALFRED CAMPBELL WALLACE was born in 1875 in Edinburgh parish, Edinburgh, Midlothian, and died in 1911 in England. He was listed as an actor at the time of his death.

MARGARET ROBERTSON must have been a real beauty and obviously held much allure for Robert. She probably had her hands full with a brood of eight children and a professionally active husband. She would have had to attend many functions and also act as hostess to many at their home in Edinburgh and later in London.

Margaret's husband ROBERT WALLACE was born of humble folk on the anniversary of the battle of Bannockburn (June 24, 1831). His father was a gardener, but with special skills. He was able to grow the best oranges, under glass, and won a silver medal from the Horticultural Society for his efforts. Early on he moved the family to Culross on the Fife coast near Kincardine where Robert enjoyed a solid education that lay the foundation for his future works. Among the many educational experiences and positions that Robert had were:

1. Educated at Geddes Institute, Cullross.

2. St. Andrew's University—Robert was a brilliant student who won 4 prizes in 1 year.

3. Private Tutor and Classics Master at Madras College, Cupar. It is here that he met, fell in love with, and married Margaret Robertson (1833).

4. Edinburgh University, Divinity Hall.

5. University of Glasgow, Doctor of Divinity (DD) in 1869.

6. Minister, Newton on Ayr Kirk, near Seafield, Ayr.

7. Minister, Trinity College Church, Edinburgh.

8. Minister, Old Greyfriar's Kirk, Edinburgh.

9. Assistant Editor of The Scotsman, Edinburgh.

10. Member of Parliament for East Edinburgh.

Of these experiences, it is probably his tenure at Old Greyfriars that is the most memorable. Probably some will remember the story of "Greyfriar's Bobby" that Disney eventually made into a film. The story, you will remember, is about a Skye Terrier called Bobby who, after the death of his master, John Gray, faithfully watched over his grave, in Old Greyfriars Kirkyard, for 14 years. In fact, when Robert assumed the position of minister at Old Greyfriars, in 1868, Bobby had already been guarding John Gray's grave for 10 years and was to be a feature in the Kirkyard, and the city of Edinburgh, for another four years, before his own death. In 1772. Bobby was buried just inside the gate of the Kirkyard, and a statue of him was built outside, some years later.

Robert was the successor to Dr. Robert Lee, who had made a name for himself as something of an independent soul, and not a true adherent to the orthodoxy of the Established Presbyterian Church in Scotland. Dr. Lee had advocated for better ways for his congregation to be involved in the service. These included standing while singing, kneeling at prayer, adornment of the Kirk with stain glass windows, and the use of an organ. Although there was much to do about Dr. Lee using these innovations, by the conservative devines of the Presbytery, the thing that raised their ire the most was the writing down of prayers and binding them in a book for common use. The General Assembly of the Kirk (governing body) went along with the innovations that Dr. Lee brought to his services, but was wishy-washy over the use of written prayers, notwithstanding the fact that there was no law against using prayers in this way. Not physically strong, Dr. Lee's health suffered and he was eventually overcome by apoplexy.

Dr. Wallace was Dr. Lee's student, and a firm believer in his approach. Those that hoped for a return to orthodoxy, with the passing of Dr. Lee were to be disappointed. Wallace quickly spawned a number of enemies who clung to the old orthodoxy. They visited his church, listened to his sermons, read and dissected them, and then wrote about them in the local newspapers, particularly the *Courant*, a Tory newspaper, and the *Daily Review,* a Disestablishers newspaper. Wallace's sermons were thoughtful, well crafted but questioned accepted doctrines like the Resurrection and the Miracles giving rise to cries of heresy. Statements like "since his (Dr. Wallace) introduction to Old Greyfriars in 1868, the whole drift of his teaching has been to assail and ridicule the fundamental doctrines of every Scottish Presbyterian denomination." And, " the incumbent of Old Greyfriars Church (Dr. Wallace) has ta'en a fee from the enemy, and soweth tares (tears) in the Lord's vineyard." Robert's diction during sermons was also attacked "His Culross pronunciation, formerly boorish and offensive is now ludicrous," and "Dr. Lee's prayers are read by Dr. Wallace in a rude, surly tone, and part of the congregation mumbles responses."

The pressure continued and those enemies of Dr. Wallace eventually forced a hearing about his activities in front of the General Assembly. In a brilliant speech, Robert refuted all that his detractors had brought to bear and he was totally exonerated by the General Assembly. Whether this episode took more of a toll on the minister than might be expected, is not really known, but he did something extraordinary. He quit the church, and his chair of Church History at Edinburgh University, essentially rejecting his ecclesiastical degree. His stand against the conservatives essentially killed off "heresy hunting in the Church of Scotland." The Assembly called the attack on Dr. Wallace an "illegal exercise of authority, and calculated to weaken the Church of Scotland and injuriously affect the right of the clergy." Still, Robert Wallace walked away.

Through contacts at Old Greyfriars, Robert secured the Assistant Editorship for the *Scotsman* newspaper. He wrote several strong opinionated editorials and one particularly against Home Rule that he felt "must not be conceded even at the risk of being scheduled as ruffians, and shot . . ." However, the hurly burly of newspaper life, the deadlines, and his own newspaper inexperience, took their toll and he resigned after four years, and left for London.

Next, he qualified for the English Bar and entered politics. He represented the Radicals of East Edinburgh in 1886, and was returned in the elections of 1892 and 1895. But, his majority began to slip, because he had lost favor with the Irish constituents, mainly due to his stand on Home Rule. He did his fair share of speech making during his time in Parliament and in the recess he visited his constituency and made long speeches about the main topics before the country. He had a small legal practice, and busied himself writing for magazines, crafting reviews, and making lectures where "his pungent humor and his sharp cynicism coupled with his knowledge of men and things, were seen to excellent advantage."

Wallace died on a June summer night while making a speech in the Commons. The air was hot that day and he had complained of losing his hearing to Sir William Arrol who was in the chamber that night. He was the first sitting MP to ever die while making a speech in the House.

Figure 8. Dr. Robert Wallace.

Robert had four brothers but was only survived by his younger brother William who was the Assistant Editor of the *Glasgow Herald* newspaper. Of his eight children five were to die prematurely including his oldest boy, Robert Lamb Wallace, who had become a barrister and had many of his father's interests. Margaret, his wife, was to die the year before Robert and her loss combined with that of his oldest son took a terrible toll on him. Robert left his small estate, valued at about 1000 pounds sterling, to his only daughter Maggie Ireland

Many felt that Robert's talents, were if not wasted, then diluted by his newspaper and political career. It was widely considered that he should have remained at Old Greyfriars and weathered the storm there, so that his true contribution could have been realized. A memorial plaque in the Kirk reads "Eminent alike for scholarship and ability, he rendered valuable service to his country in the various positions he occupied."

When I found the name Dr. Wallace and a connection with Old Greyfriars' Church, I requested some information from the church about him. Padi Mathieson, Publications Officer at the Kirk sent me a lot of information together with a quip "I am surprised that you know so little of your famous forebear as he played a very important part in the religious and intellectual affairs in Scotland in the 19th century."

DAVID ROBERTSON, James's seventh child, was born March 18, 1841, Cupar, Fife, and died November 13, 1868, Cupar, Fife.

David was a tanner for a short time probably until his older brother Andrew took over the family business and then David joined him. He was to be struck down early by tuberculosis, the same disease that took his brother Peter.

David was also a sergeant in the Volunteer Corps in Cupar. On December 3, 1868 the following notice appeared in the *Fifeshire Journal*:

"Death of Sergeant David Robertson—We regret to have to announce the death of Sergeant Robertson of No I Company, who has been cut off after a considerable period of delicate health, in the prime of his youth. His kindness of heart and his enthusiasm in the Volunteer cause greatly endeared him to the whole Corps, in the prosperity of which he took a deep interest, while so long as health was given to him he was most regular and assiduous in the discharge of his duties, and his loss will be much felt by all ranks. In token of their respect, his remains are to be accompanied to their last resting place by the Corps tomorrow, at two o'clock."

David left a will with an assessment of 510 pounds sterling. This was based on a Life Assurance Policy from the North British and Mercantile Insurance Co. for 500 pounds, and for a silver watch and "body clothes." All his effects were bequeathed to his mother who was appointed executor. John Lumsden, shopman to Mrs. Robertson, was the witness.

CHAPTER 6

ANDREW ROBERTSON (5G), was born August 22, 1836 in Cupar, Fife, and died October 18, 1881 in Cupar, Fife. He married JANET THALLON March 31, 1864 in Cupar, Fife, daughter of HENRY THALLON and AGNES MILLER. She was born 1838 in Smithygreen, Leven, Fife, and died June 30, 1924 in 10 Dalhousie Terrace, Morningside, Edinburgh.

Andrew and Janet had four children AGNES born 1866, MAGGIE born 1867, ANNIE HAY born 1869 and JAMES born 1872.

LIFE AND TIMES OF ANDREW ROBERTSON:
In *Fife Shopkeepers and Traders* by Campbell vol. 2, Cupar— Andrew was listed as the "second" son who took over the business at 21 Bonnygate from his mother and sister (probably Anne) after the death of his father.

Once Andrew took over the family business, he was also recruited to stand for the Town Council, like his father before him. In October 1879, *The Fifeshire Journal* reported that Andrew was elected with six others to the Town Council, following a large turnout at the polls.

The *1881 census* indicates that Andrew, his wife Janet, their four children and house servant Agnes Braid (26 years from Bonnyton, Fife) were all living at 21 Bonnygate, Cupar, Fife, Scotland. He was a master flesher and employed two men, one boy and one female.

Andrew was known around the county as a great cricketer playing for Scotland XIs versus England XIs. *Scotland Cricket* could not confirm that Andrew played for his country in these early years of the recorded game. Apparently there were many unofficial games that he probably played in. Unfortunately, Andrew was also something of an alcoholic that went unchecked for at least six years, eventually contributing to his early demise when he was only 45.

At the time of his death, Andrew's estate was worth 1,815 pounds sterling. He was also owed just under 1000 pounds by several fairly

well to do clients like Lady Campbell of Dura, the Reverend
Johnstone of Leuchars, Provost James Hain, Colonel George and
Lady Baxter. He still had the six shares in Cupar Gas that were worth
about 150 pounds, a Policy of Insurance with the North British &
Mercantile Insurance company worth 624 pounds sterling. He also
had about 16 pounds in the National Bank of Scotland in Cupar.
Andrew had lent securities to Robert Milne, farmer and Mr. Milne
had assigned to Andrew a Policy of Insurance on his life for 200
pounds as a bond of cash credit. Janet, Andrew's wife was named as
executor and took over the running of the business.

JANET THALLON ROBERTSON, Andrew's wife, disposed of
the butcher business to Thomas Auld in May 1882. She was living at
Westfield Park, Westerlea, Cupar in 1891 with her daughter Sophia
and son James. James was a bank clerk at the time. Janet was then
living on private means, following the death of her husband.

The *1901 census* shows Janet living at the Morningside address in
Edinburgh with her two spinster daughters Agnes Sophia (35 years)
and Annie Hay (32 years), together with her widowed daughter
Margaret Simpson (34 years) and her son George Archibald Simpson
(nine years). There is no mention of Janet's son James who would
have been 29 years. He was last known to have been working as a
bank clerk in Cupar, probably for the National Bank of Scotland who
also employed his uncle James as an examiner.

Janet died in 1924 at 88 years a victim of arteriosclerosis and
chronic myocarditis. She was still living at her Morningside address.
No will could be found in her name following her death.

AGNES SOPHIA ROBERTSON, Andrew's first child, born in
Cupar, probably never married, but her name appears in the *1891
census* living at Westfield Park in Cupar, with her mother. In 1901
she was still living with her mother, this time in Morningside,
Edinburgh. Thereafter, her name could not be traced.

Andrew's second child MAGGIE IRELAND ROBERTSON was also born in Cupar and she died April 1, 1956, 37 Lygon Road, Edinburgh of cardiovascular degeneration.

Maggie married GEORGE SIMPSON April 14, 1889 in Cupar, Fife. He was born about 1860 in Shotts, Lanarkshire, and died August 5, 1889 in Edinburgh. George was a Presbyterian minister in Stirling.

The *1891 census* indicates that George, his wife Maggie (Margaret) and housekeeper Martha B. Dickison (born in Linlithgow) were living at Airth Parish Manse. Airth is banked by the Firth of Forth and the parishes of Kinnar, Larbet, and St. Ninians. Airth is thought to have stemmed from the Gaelic "Ard" signifying a hill. A description of the church states that it was "a very handsome little structure, containing accommodation for 800 sitters, and the manse seated on rising ground a little distance from the village (of Airth). All of these tend, not little, to adorn the scenery on the south banks of the Forth, between Kincardine and Alloa."

In 1892 GEORGE ARHIBALD DUNDAS SIMPSON was born, the only child of George and Margaret. Nothing is known of what happened to George (junior). He did not sign his mother's death certificate in 1956, and his name fails to appear in any of the available documents.

When George (senior) died in 1899, in Edinburgh, he left a young wife and child. His estate was worth 1,472 pounds sterling including two Life Insurance Policies with the Norwich Union for almost 1000 pounds and a residual amount from his incumbency.

George, in his will, bid his wife to "be Tutor and Curator to my child or children while in minority." Maggie decided that life would be easier nearer family and decided to stay in Edinburgh, permanently, soon after George's funeral. Maggie died in 1956 (88 years) at Lygon Road in Edinburgh, but no will could be found.

ANNIE HAY ROBERTSON, Andrew's third child, was born June 27, 1869 also in Cupar.

She married CHARLES WOOD November 20, 1901 in 10 Dalhousie Terrace, Newington, Edinburgh, son of WILLIAM WOOD and JANET WILKINSON. He was born 1874 and died 1953 in Kirkaldy Hospital, Fife. The marriage certificate shows Annie's age to be 27 years but in fact she was 32 years.

CHARLES WOOD was listed as a solicitor, in 1901, with a residence at 19 Union Street, Edinburgh. When Charles Wood died he had moved his home from Edinburgh to Kirkaldy. It is not clear if he was still practicing law during his time in Kirkaldy. He died of congestive cardiac failure. Annie and Charles Wood had one child A. THALLON WOOD. He appears as the signee to his father's death certificate and was listed as living at 32 Whytehouse Avenue, Kirkaldy in 1953. No records could be found of his birth or a marriage.

Andrew's only son, JAMES ROBERTSON, was born on October 17, 1872 in Cupar. He did not follow his father into the fleshing business. Instead in 1891, he was listed as a bank clerk living at Westfield Park in Cupar, with his mother. He, or another family member, may have decided that the banking business might offer more opportunities than butchering. What happened to him is unknown. He was not living with his mother in Edinburgh 10 years later and no marriage record or death certificate could be located. However, James Robertson was a very common name in the early 1900s, and his name might have been missed. Since he seemed to be following the career path of his uncle James, working in London, a search was made for his name south of the border, but it failed to turn up in any of the available family papers.

CHAPTER 7

JAMES ROBERTSON (5G), was born July 14, 1839 in Cupar, Fife, and died March 31, 1907 in Hampstead, London. He married MARGARET ELIZABETH McVEAGH August 31, 1871 in Southfield, Liberton, Edinburgh, daughter of JOHN McVEAGH and JESSIE CROALL. She was born 1847 in Middlesex, London, and died 1906 in 11 Chesterford Gardens, Hampstead, Middlesex.

James and Margaret had five children <u>PATRICK</u> born 1872, *JESSIE* born 1873, *ELSIE* born 1875, MAUD born 1878 and <u>RONALD</u> born 1883. Both Patrick and Ronald carried the Robertson name forwards.

Life and Times of JAMES ROBERTSON.

James was quite successful in his banking career and made a lot of friends. The *1881 census* indicates that James' wife Maggie, and four of her five children were residing at 23 Mayfield Terrace, Edinburgh. James was not listed and may have been away on business that night. There were also three servants listed, Catherine McLeod (25 years), Johan Menzies (22 years), Annie Munro (19 years). All servants were born in the North of Scotland. In the same year James left for London. He and his wife were presented with a "Service of Silver Plate" and "a diamond ring for Mrs. Robertson." The presentation was made by Arthur Morrison of the National Bank of Scotland, Edinburgh. Part of the written sentiment from Mr. Morrison read as follows:

"I feel fure I echo the feeling of every Subfciber, that you carry with you to your new home their beft wifthes for your future welfare, and their fincere hope that Mrs. Robertson and you may enjoy continued profperity and great happinef, and be long fpared to each other."

(Notice the old English use of the letter "f" for an "s.")

June Robertson (1928) indicates that MARGARET McVEAGH was the belle of Edinburgh and was much sought after by eligible bachelors before her marriage to James. The marriage was to last for another 26 years before the untimely death of Margaret Robertson who, late at night, fell to her death after tripping over the family pet, a Scottie, at the head of a flight of stairs. At the time, the Robertsons

47

were living at Chesterfield Gardens in Hampstead. James was heartbroken by the event and died within the next year, in 1907. Margaret would have inherited everything, but because of her earlier death James, in his will, divided everything among his children and friends.

Figure 9. James Robertson 'the banker' (c 1880).

The house in which they were living was sizable as the will identifies many rooms in which items were to be found. A main bedroom, spare bedroom, books bedroom, and a servant bedroom are mentioned. There was also a morning room, a billiard room, a dining room, and a drawing room, beside the more mundane areas like the kitchen, scullery, and bathrooms. What strikes you about the will is the listing of art items of which there are at least 55 separate pieces. There were images of James and Margaret in marble and also in cotta busts. There were painted portraits of the couple, and two other portraits of Margaret alone. These were all divided up among the

Figure 10. Portrait of Margaret McVeah (c 1880).

children. The art collection was varied consisting of an image of Robert Burns, a picture of Skye, a picture of "Man in Boat," and a picture of an "Old Man and Old Lady." There were also works by Llewellyn, Constable, and local works by Gribble. Patrick received James's curling stones, and Ronald the "Armour in the Hall," Jessie got an "Eagle Mirror," Elsie a piano. All three daughters shared in the division of the silver. James's stock holdings were quite varied and included Koffyfontein Mines Ltd, United Horse Shop and Nail Co, London and Denver Mining Corporation, Nigeria and West Africa Development Syndicate, the Libiola Copper Mining Co. At least 14 holdings were in mining with the bulk in the gold sector. James also bought an interest in the "Down to Earth" Borough of Hampstead Cemetery as he laid the foundation for his eternal rest.

One thing that James did, in his will, was to order the sale of the contents of his wine cellar and cigar cabinet. Both Patrick and Ronald enjoyed cigars and Patrick enjoyed some drink, too, so the loss of these items was deeply felt by the boys.

Also, James did provide for Louisa Spikins, called "Spik," who had been a faithful servant during the formative years of the Robertson children, in London. She received "the bedroom clock in the morning room, the small table, the two small chairs, the chest of drawers in the bathroom, and the furniture in the Books Bedroom and her own bed." Spik used to threaten the children with "I will tell your father" when things got out of hand, but she never followed through.

Figure 11. James Robertson in highland attire.
Inverness (c 1895).

JESSIE EVA ROBERTSON, the second child of James and
Margaret, was born December 4, 1873 in Edinburgh, and died March
27, 1949 in Dunblane, Perth of pneumonia. She married HUGH
WALLACE AITKEN April 2, 1903 in St. Mary's, Kilburn,
Hampstead, London. He was born 1865 in Glasgow, and died 1947 in
Torburn, Bearsden.

They had four children WALLACE born 1904, KENNETH born
1905, MALCOLM born 1907, and DOUGLAS born 1911.

EVA had the distinction of being baptized in Old Greyfriars Kirk
in Edinburgh, December 31st, 1873. She lived in several places during
her life including Edinburgh, London, Bearsden, Glasgow, and finally
Dunblane. Her marriage to Hugh Aitken was not a happy one and the
couple separated around 1922, when Eva moved to Glasgow with her
son Wallace. She is remembered as being a very elegant lady, slim
and fond of fanciful hats.

Figure 12. Hugh Aitken & Eva Robertson (c 1908).

When Eva died her estate was worth 2,183 pounds, and the bulk of it went to her son Wallace. Eva obviously liked jewelry, which she passed around to her relatives. Wallace (1904) received her three stone diamond engagement ring and gold watch bracelet. Malcolm (1907) received a sapphire and diamond half hoop ring and a sapphire and diamond cross over ring. Eilla, Wallace's wife, received a pearl and gold dress chain, a silver traveling clock, and a silver topped powder jar. Margorie (1905) had a long gold dress chain with locket and a slave bangle. Elsie, Eva's sister, received a diamond wrist watch, a diamond and Amethyst Roblun brooch, a crocodile dressing case, cherub silver hair brush, clothes brush and hand glass, an emerald and diamond bar brooch and all Eva's personal clothing. Ronald, her brother, received his mother's (Margaret) gold Keyser ring. Spik, the long suffering family retainer, received a cherub silver workbox and Gordon brooch.

HUGH WALLACE AITKEN, Eva's husband, was a colonial engineer and sugar machinery specialist. He was schooled at the Glasgow Academy and Anderson's College. He founded the firm of Aitken and Company, Colonial Engineers, in Glasgow. He designed machinery used to crush cane and make sugar. Many of his patents were taken up in sugar producing countries and he was abroad on many occasions. In 1929 Hugh retired form active business practice.

Ian Aiken (1936) remembers that Hugh climbed to the top of the Forth Rail Bridge in the late 1880s, and that he set high standards for his sons. His home in Bearsden had lovely gardens that were enjoyed by all who visited him.

WALLACE AITKEN , Eva's first child, was born March 4, 1904 at 21 Falkland Mansions, Kelvinside, Glasgow, and died December 23, 1971. He married EILLA MABEL LAIRD December 1, 1937 in Dunblane, Scotland. She was born 1905, and died 1992.

Wallace and Eilla had two children IONA LAIRD born 1947 and GARY ROBERTSON born 1949.

Following his schooling at Glasgow Academy, WALLACE entered the engineering program at Glasgow University in October 1923, but had to withdraw due to contracting tuberculosis. At that time he was living with his mother in Glasgow, following her separation from Hugh Aitken. Wallace was hospitalized in Aberdeen at Tornader where his treatment required him to lie on a bed outside in the elements. Later, he was sent to Switzerland to recuperate and eventually returned to Scotland to live with his mother at Loan Park in Dunblane.

Iona Leggat (1947) recounts that when Wallace and Eilla Laird started going out, Eilla's father was not keen on his daughter going out with this delicate young man with no job. Eilla was sent to India to visit her aunt who happened to be the wife of the Bishop of Nagpur. The hope was that the separation from Wallace would cool Eilla's feelings, but that was not to be. They were married and the reception was held at the Laird's family home "Crawford Park" in

Dunblane. While the guests were waiting for the bride and groom to leave, the young couple climbed out of a back window to avoid the fuss.

Wallace was a tall man (6 foot 2 inches), slim, with a charming personality. He enjoyed golf and curling in his spare time. During his tenure as an hotelier, he also cared for his mother, father-in-law, and the sister of his father-in-law at the hotel, in Dunblane, until they passed on.

IONA LAIRD AITKEN, Wallace's first child, married JOHN BRIAN LEGGAT in 1972. He was born 1948.
They have two children JAMES DOUGLAS, born 1982, and JOANNA RACHEL, born 1983.

GARRY ROBERTSON AITKEN, Wallace's second child married (1) JANE ANNE FINLAYSON STRATHDEE. She was born 1950, and they have one child STEVEN DAMIAN born in 1975
He married (2) ANNE McGREGOR in 1979, and they have two children SCOTT GREGOR, born in 1984, and ROSS GARRY, born in 1985.

KENNETH AITKEN, Eva's second child, was born March 6, 1905, and died August 19, 1944, near Caen, Normandy during WW2.

Kenneth was educated first at the Glasgow Academy, and later received a degree from the Glasgow Royal Technical College (in mechanical engineering). He was captain of cricket and held the high jump record at the Academy. At the outbreak of war he enlisted with the Royal Artillery and was at Dunkirk. Then he was with the 153rd Infantry Brigade of the 51st Highland Division, and was awarded the Military Cross at Mareth. He was killed in France in 1944 when he was a major. He was described as "an officer of outstanding courage and devotion to duty."

MALCOLM AITKEN, Eva's third child was born September 29, 1907 and died December 17, 1999. He married MARGORIE WINIFRED JUDD in 1935. She was born 1905.

Malcolm and Margorie have two children IAN MALCOLM born 1936 and HAMISH WILSOUN born 1939.

Malcolm was also educated at the Glasgow Academy and played rugby and fives. Malcolm's niece Iona remembers him as a quiet and kind man with a lovely sense of humor. He and his wife Marjorie owned a caravette in which they toured extensively around Scotland.

Hamish Aitken (1939) remembers his father as loving mountaineering and golf and having a rugby football trial for Scotland at fly half (like a quarter back in US football). During the war he was a Captain in the Highland Light Infantry. After the war he worked for Balfour Beatty, a heavy engineering company, as a chartered accountant until his retirement. Hamish remembers that his mother (Marjorie) and father enjoyed an idyllically happy marriage over 64 years—"a lesson in love and stability to us all." The excursions of the couple in their caravette allowed Malcolm to fish and Marjorie to paint. She was a member of the ladies section of the Royal Scottish Academy.

IAN MALCOLM AITKEN, the first son of Malcolm and Margorie, married HAZEL F. LOCK. She was born 1942.
Ian and Hazel had four children. MAIRI ELAINE ZOE , born 1964. She lived only two days. KENNETH MALCOLM HAROLD was born 1965.
FERGUS SHAUN WALLACE was born 1967. He married FIONA ELIZABETH McCALLUM 1997. She was born 1969.
Fergus and Fiona have two children SOPHIE GEMMA born 1999, and FINLAY JAMES LEWIS, born 2001.
TRISTAN FRANCIS IAN AITKEN, Ian and Hazel's last child, was born 1971. He married ELIZABETH GALLAGHER 1992. She was born 1964. They have two children PHILIP RUIRIADH BRADEN , born 1996, and CHLOE BRIANNA AMBER , born 1998

HAMISH WILSOUN AITKEN the second son of Malcolm and Marjorie Aitken was born 1939. He married CAROLYN BETTY ALLEN 1970. She was born 1943.

Hamish and Carolyn have two children DOUGLAS WILSOUN born 1972 in Rhodesia and ROBERT MALCOLM born 1974, in England.

Hamish was schooled at Edinburgh Academy and Gordonstoun. He qualified as a chartered accountant of Scotland in 1963 and then worked his way around the world for a 100 pounds bet. He then returned to Medical School at St. Mary's in London, qualified in 1971 and took up general practice in Forest Row, Sussex (1975-1999).

Hamish recounts that he met his wife-to-be Carolyn while skiing in Italy in 1963. He pursued her to Australia, but it took him five more years to convince her to marry him. He owns a near ruined croft house in the west highlands and gave Carolyn a real loo (lavatory) with running water and a stove as a wedding present. The cottage is his "spiritual home where he fishes, stalks (red deer) and communes with nature." It takes 11 hours and 10 minutes to drive the 625 miles from his Sussex home to the croft that is still without electricity.

DOUGLAS ATKEN, Hamish and Carolyn's first son, was educated first at Eastbourne College and then Leicester University. Although he started medicine at Eatbourne, he left and spent 18 months in Malawi running a hotel for travelers and then returned home and completed his medical studies. He lived with at his grandmother, Margorie Judd (1905), in Edinburgh, caring for her during the last part of her life. He is a Shiatsu practitioner, a teacher of Tai Chi, and enjoys gardening and green wood carpentry.

ROBERT AITKEN, Hamish and Carolyn's second child, like his brother, was also educated at Eastbourne College and Leicester University. Robert graduated from Leicester with a degree in Psychology. He traveled to Argentina for a wedding that did not materialize and then took a year to come home. He hitched to Tierra del Fuego to swim in the Beagle Channel and then climbed a glacier. He then headed for warmer climates and hitched to Colombia to swim in the Caribbean.

On his return he joined a publishing company in London. His latest claim to fame was achieving a place in the Guinness Book of Records for the highest formal dinner party in the world. This involved climbing 23,000 feet (Lhakpa Ri coming up from Everest advanced base camp) carrying table, chairs, food, candelabra, and sitting down to a four-course dinner wearing top hat, white tie, and tails. He wore his Glengarry and kilt. Robert recently married VIRGINIE DURLOT.

DOUGLAS AITKEN, the fourth son of Eva and Hugh Aitken, was born April 20, 1911 and died October 16, 1935.

Douglas had an extensive education at the Glasgow Academy, Sedbergh, Caius College Cambridge and Glasgow University. He won a Blue for rugby while at Cambridge and while at Glasgow won two medals for his work in medicine. He had hoped to marry a young lady named Jean Hendry, but he tragically died of pneumonia, in 1934, while studying medicine at Glasgow. His epitaph from the university read "No one who came in contact with Douglas Aiken could fail to be charmed by his frankness, modesty, and imperturbable good nature."

He died the year before the availability of penicillin.

ELSIE ROBERTSON, the third child of James and Margaret Robertson was born May 17, 1875, Edinburgh and died between February-March 1954, Hampstead, London. She married (1) SIR WILLIAM ARROL, November 16, 1910, Kilmadock, Perth. He was born 1839, Houston, Renfrewshire, Scotland and died February 20, 1913, Seafield, near Ayr, Scotland. Elsie married (2) SIR ROBERT JOHN COLLIE in 1928 in Hampstead, London, and he was born in 1860, Aberdeen, and died April 4, 1935, 42 Porchester Terrace, London W2.

June Robertson (1928) reports that Elsie was very passionate over her Scottish roots that may have explained her marriages to two famous Scotsmen. She was very autocratic which brought her into head-on collisions with May Wills (1889), the wife of her brother Ronald, resulting in a feud that lasted all their lives. She could also be very generous to those that mattered to her. Except for her brief marriages to Sir William Arrol and Sir Robert Collie Elsie probably lived with her sister Maud at the Finchley Road address in Hampstead.

SIR WILLIAM ARROL, Elsie's first husband, was born in 1839 in Houston, Renfrewshire the son of a cotton spinner. At nine years he worked as a "piercer" at a cotton mill in Johnstone. In 1850 he moved to Paisley and worked at Coates Thread Manufactory, and then apprenticed as a blacksmith while learning mathematics at night school from a weaver, in his shop. He worked as a journeyman on the Clyde shipyard, then at a number of related jobs, until he landed a job as a foreman at Laidlaws Engineering Works in Glasgow at a salary of two pounds a week.

By 1872 he had struck out on his own and built his famous Iron Works at Dalmarnock. In 1875 he built the North British Railway Bridge over the Clyde at Bothwell. The Caledonian Bridge followed this over the Clyde at the Broomielaw, in Glasgow.. Then came his two greatest feats, the New Tay Bridge in 1882 and the Forth Rail Bridge in 1890. When he was building both bridges he had a hugely demanding schedule. During the weekdays he would rise at 5a.m. and arrive at Dalmarnock at 6 a.m. to review the days work on both bridges. At 8:45 a.m. he would take the train to Edinburgh to work on the Forth Bridge, then at 6 p.m. he would take the train to Dundee to inspect the Tay site, but always took the late train back to Glasgow for the next mornings work. On Friday nights he would take the train to London to confer with engineers about both jobs and return to Glasgow on Saturday. In his spare time, he also invented a hydraulic riveting machine that could clench seven rivets in a minute.
{Here is a good party question - how many rivets are there on the Forth Rail Bridge? Answer 6. 5 million, weighing 4,200 tons.}
William's bridge building feats resulted in world acclaim and a knighthood. He went on to build other bridges like the Tower Bridge in London, three bridges over the Nile at Cairo, and the North Bridge in Edinburgh.

Arrol was not a speech making person but when forced to do so, he often reminisced about his humble origins. As the years passed he lamented on the trend of the younger generation to garner more education than their fathers, and the prevailing thought that this education elevated them to the class of a gentleman. In a speech, in Ayr, he commented "I held it altogether wrong that so many men are not learning trades. Give them, certainly, the best education that you can, but at the same time give them a trade along with their education." Sir William saw the developing problems that would later beset many industrial countries.

Sir William was also a loyal Liberal Unionist MP (Member of Parliament) for South Ayrshire for 14 years. The *1901 census* in Scotland indicates that Sir William and his then wife Elizabeth Pattison (born in Paisley, Scotland) were living in a 24-room house in Seafield, Ayr. They had one servant Jane Weir from Aberdeen. Elizabeth, who had mental issues for several years died in 1903. In 1905 Sir William then married his cousin Jessie Hodgart. On his wedding day he was informed that there was a vote to break a division within the House of Commons. Without waiting for the reception he took his new wife and boarded a train for London. Arriving late in the evening he sped across town to arrive just in time to cast his vote. In recognition of his loyalty to the Party, the Prime Minister, A.J. Balfour, presented Sir William with a silver cup with the inscription "for conspicuous loyalty."

What Jessie thought about all this is not recorded. Jessie too, passed on and in 1910 Sir William married Elsie Robertson. William may have known Elsie's brother-in-law Robert Wallace when he was a young minister at Newton On Ayr, since his parish was close to Sir William's home in Seafield. Later, Robert was an MP for East Edinburgh, and it is very likely the pair would have known each other both professionally and socially. Elsie would likely have been introduced at some time during their exchanges.

Figure 13. Sir William Arrol.

Witnesses to the Arrol marriage included Elsie's sister Maud and brother Ronald. Elsie listed the Finchley Road address as her normal residence. Kilmadock, the Parish in which the marriage took place, lies between Dunblane and Callandar within the Burugh of Doune. The location is very near the picturesque Trossachs, an area frequented, in the past, by the famous outlaw Rob Roy McGregor. It would have been a very attractive location for a summer honeymoon, but this was November. Why marry in a location that must have been difficult to get to and would probably be experiencing inclement weather? The answer is probably in Elsie's father's will. James (1839) had a great friend in Doune, George Sutherland Mackey, who was remembered in James's will with two small water colours by "RG." George just happened to be minister of the United Free Church in Doune, and I suspect that Elsie's fierce nationalistic pride combined with the strong family connection with George was sufficient to motivate her to arrange a Scottish location for the marriage.

By the time Elsie married Sir William most of his great bridge building exploits were complete. He was a wealthy man but was 36 years senior to Elsie, and was to live for only three years following their marriage. He died of bronchial pneumonia. In his will Sir William left almost 338,000 pounds (relative worth today is about 118 million pounds). He must have been a very generous man, he took care financially, of all his relatives, and the relatives of his former wives and their children. He helped some not-so-near relatives and his various servants and his chauffeur. He left 10,000 pounds in trust for his estate administrators to distribute to those that he "might have forgotten" or those "who were in need." He had two additional homes other than his Seafield mansion, one in Paisley (Merklerriggs) and the other in Kilmacolm. Sir William allowed family members to live rent free in these homes with free range of all the contents. He held a number of different stocks including the North British Locomotive Co. Ltd and the Clyde Shipbuilding and Engineering Co., but had also invested in the new steamships including Strathay, Strathspey and Strathness Steamship Companies. He also bequeathed his Gatehouse at the Seafield estate to his gardener John McCartney and his family, and also provided annuities to pay for duty and taxes on the home of the nieces of his late brother John, at Eastlands, Craigmore. He provided multiple sums to many organizations including 2,500 pounds to Glasgow Royal Infirmary and Glasgow Western Infirmary. 1000 pounds to the University of Glasgow and 1000 pounds Glasgow Old Men's Friend Society, and the Old Women's Home.

After Sir William's death, Elsie was financially secure. By his will she received a 5000 pounds down payment and an annuity of 1,200 pounds. She retained all her jewelry, and could choose any of the materials in the Seafield estate (a 24 room mansion with grounds) in Ayr. That included "all consumable stores, carriage horses and harnesses, furnishings and plenishings," valued at 16,800 pounds, and she also shared in the residual estate.

Figure 14. One of the three cantilever towers of the Forth rail bridge. A tower of the Forth road bridge is in the background (c 1990).

SIR ROBERT JOHN COLLIE, Elsie's second husband, was born in Pitfodles, Aberdeenshire. He was one of five brothers and a sister. He was admitted to Aberdeen University and graduated with an MD in 1885. It was not long before he decided to travel south and was to make London his home. He held a number of important positions including Chief Medical Officer for the Metropolitan Water Board, Consultant Medical Officer to the Ministry of Pensions, Vice President Medico-Legal Society, Temporary Honorary Colonel AMS (Army Medical Service), and Director of Medical Services at the Ministry of Pensions. He wrote a number of professional books including—*Fraud and Detection in Accident Insurance Claims*; 1912, *Malingering and Feigned Sickness*, 1913; the *Psychology of the Fraudulent Mind;* and *Fraud in Medico-Legal Practice*, 1932.

He was highly respected for his work on malingering and assessments of workers fitness to return to work, particularly following accidents. He is still quoted today in the research literature on the topic of malingering. Sir Robert had great skill in reaching the truth about individual cases, and came up with a figure of 8% of those that he examined that he said were malingerers. Most problems about not wanting to return to work, he found, were psychological. He felt that some workers "brooded" over their injuries and giving them compensation, took away the stimulus to work. Collie helped form the Workers Compensation Act in 1906 that ensured a medical assessor's participation in the process. Before WW1 he had participated in 31,000 consecutive medical exams over a nine-year period. He was involved in the "Telegraphers Cramp Epidemic" of 1912 when about 60% of the workforce came down with symptoms of fatigue and some nervous complaints. Collie was able to save thousands of pounds in wages and rescued others from the "ill effects of unnecessary protracted invalidism." Malingerers at that time were classified as real, partial, or sub conscious. He was knighted in 1912 for his efforts.

Collie carried his professional interests into WW1 when dealing with shell shock victims suffering from functional Nervous Disorder (or Neurasthenia). Sir Robert scorned academics and psychoanalysts who wanted to treat this condition with things other than "common sense." He said, "personally, I have always believed that hard work and continuous work is the only way to be really happy, and that in one form or another is the only salvation for those who are suffering from functional Nervous Disorder." He felt that Neurasthenia was mostly self- induced with patients prone to weak wills and "morbid introspection." His treatment was to "capture the mind quickly, then set it in the right mould" by surrounding patients with positive attitudes and providing outdoor labour whenever possible.

He had his detractors who labeled him as "less a specialist than a monomaniac," with "an obsessive interest in the detection of malingering," and motivated with "high handed, spiteful careerism." A friend wrote of him "It would, perhaps, be not quite correct to describe Collie as a typical Aberdonian Soul, but he had a dogged honesty of mind and a contempt for humbug, he was courageous and fearless. A certain combativeness made him a "bonnie fechter" (good fighter)." Sir Robert was made CMG (Companion of Order of St. Michael and St. George) and was also a Justice of the Peace (JP).

In 1922 Collie became an MP for Partick in Glasgow, but was not recognized for his abilities as a politician. He was very outspoken, but took little trouble to appease those that disagreed with him. This gave him something of a "Dr. Jekel and Mr. Hyde" reputation.

In 1928 Sir Robert's first wife Jessie Edgar died, and within the same year he married Elsie (Robertson) Arrol in Hampstead. Elsie had been a widow for 15 years and Robert was 15 years her senior. It is not clear how the two met but they may have moved in the same social circles and Elsie may have been attracted to him because of his Scottish heritage and his "bulldog" approach to things that mattered. Certainly, she was unlikely to have been attracted by any financial motives, since Sir William Arrol had left her financially sound.

Their marriage lasted about seven years until Sir Robert died in his Bayswater home. His will is illuminating as it may shed some light on his feelings about those closest to him. His son, by an earlier arrangement, received most of his cash. Mary Wright, his live-in secretary at Porchester Terrace, received a 200 pounds legacy for life for her "loyal, untiring and faithful service." She shared in the division of the house furnishing and trappings and also received a 100 pounds fee as one of the executors of the estate. Sir Robert left financial awards for most of his friends and relatives. He left a special award of 1000 pounds, in trust, for his grandson Ian Collie to further his medical studies and education. His chauffeur, Arthur Oldham, received 500 pounds, his overcoat, clothes and a dressing case and his Rolls Royce motor car. His gardener, Graham Boorman, received 30 pounds but did not get his motor mower or garden tools—they went on to the auction block. It seemed that Sir Robert wanted to bestow gifts in order to "recognize those who have honoured me with their affection and above all their true loyalty."

Conspicuously absent from the will was the name of Elsie Collie. She received one mention when Sir Robert requested that his executors send "Lady Arrol" a copy of the will, and that was all. His sentiments toward his two wives may perhaps best be found in his provision toward the Royal National Lifeboat Institution for one-third of his residual estate. He also added this:

"I EXPRESS a wish (but without imposing any legal obligation on the said Institution) that in consideration of the aforementioned bequest, the National Lifeboat Institution will within three years of my death name one of the boats built by it "Jessie Edgar," in memory of the Love I bore to a gentle soul and one whose saintly life I cherish to my death, whose sincerity, disinterested love and devotion were for 42 years past all telling and who, had she survived me would have inherited the whole of my fortune."

Figure 15. Sir Robert Collie.

Elsie was not to marry again, and lived the rest of her life off the Finchley Road in Hampstead, London. It seems that Elsie also preferred the name of Arrol to Collie, and after Robert's death, she was referred to as "Lady Arrol" or "Elsie R. Arrol." When she died she left a considerable fortune and 57 persons received legacies in her will. These legacies came from the cash sale of all Elsie's personal property. June Robertson (1928), states that Elsie considered none of the Robertson women "worthy enough" to wear her jewelry and it was all sold together with her clothes and furniture.

The redoubtable "Spik," (Louise Sipkins) receive an annuity of 52 pounds. "Spik" seems to have been remembered by all her former charges. Elsie also left legacies to person linked with philanthropic societies like the Red Cross, London Missionary Society, Glengall Mental Hospital in Ayr, Royal Alexandra Infirmary in Paisley, near Glasgow. These were usually accompanied by an enjoinder that she hoped the named person would use the money for their own needs.

Since the 1930s, Elsie had been secretary to the Hepburn Starey Blind Aid Society and she left 300 pounds to be shared among the oldest members and her "special friends." She also left some cash for those that came and "entertained" her blind friends. Out of her residual estate she bequeathed the Society and additional 1000 pounds "to help with the affairs of the Society," and for "seaside holidays."

A surprise recipient of a legacy of 1000 pounds was Sir Alexander Fleming, the discoverer of penicillin. The legacy seems to have been in recognition of the man's work. Elsie might have known Sir Alexander through her husband, Sir Robert Collie. During WW1 Sir Alexander was a Captain in the Army Medical Corps, and, at that time, Collie would have been his commanding officer. Fleming died about a year after Elsie, of a sudden heart attack, having spent most of his professional life at St. Mary's Hospital in Paddington, London.

The bulk of the legacies, and portions of the cash from Elsie's residual estate, were shared among the families of Patrick Robertson, Eva Robertson and Ronald Robertson. The way the pie was cut up probably speaks volumes as to the level of esteem that Elsie held the different family units. Eva Robertson's immediate family received eight times more than Pat's, and Ronald's family received 16 times the amount bequeathed to Pat's family.

MAUD ROBERTSON, the fourth child of James and Margaret Robertson, was born November 13, 1878, Edinburgh Parish, Edinburgh, Midlothian, and died about 1944, London, England.

Maud remained a spinster living in Hampstead. After leaving the family home in Chesterfield Gardens, after the death of her father James (1839), she probably lived at the same address off the Finchley Road until her death. This was probably a flat (apartment) that she shared with her sister Elsie. Elsie would have been absent during her two, relatively brief, marriages.

Maud was known as "chips" to her family and she was devoted to her brother Ronald (1883) and kept a scrap book of all his various athletic endeavours. She used to send my father Douglas (1903) post cards from trips that she used to take with Elsie. Mostly pictures of Scottish soldiers or castles. She may have had something of a weight problem as she sometimes referred to her large size in the post cards. She seemed to be in attendance at all the important family functions— her brother Ronald's marriage to Mary Wills; Elsie's marriage to Sir William Arrol in Doune; she also signed Sir William's death certificate; and she was probably in attendance at Elsie's marriage to Sir Robert Collie, in Hampstead. She was something of a painter as she had at least two pictures hanging in the old Chesterfield Gardens family home. However, her father James (1839) bequeathed them back to her in his will, so they may have been of questionable quality. Maud may have made a most favorable impression on Sir William Arrol, because he left her 5000 pounds in his will, enough for her to live comfortably in her apartment.

CHAPTER 8

PATRICK JAMES ROBERTSON (6G) was born July 25, 1872 in Newington, Edinburgh, and died January 23, 1961 at 11 Well Road, Hampstead, London. He married MABEL WILHELMINA DESPARD June 2, 1903 in Hampstead, London, England, daughter of WILLAM FREDERICK DESPARD. She was born 1872 in St. John, Hampstead , Middlesex, and died 1926 in Hampstead, London.

Patrick and Mabel had three children DOUGLAS born in 1904, AILLEN born 1910, and MARION born in 1915. Douglas was to carry the Robertson family name forwards.

Life and times of PATRICK JAMES ROBERTSON:

Pat, as he was known, like his brother Ronald was a good sportsman. He played 1st XI cricket in 1889 and 1890 while attending Highgate School in Hampstead. After leaving school he played soccer for the London-Scottish Club, and was an excellent golfer. He used wooden shafted clubs – a driver, 3 iron, 5 iron, a mashe-niblic, and a putter and won most of the competitions that he entered. He was fond of scoffing at his opponents who would appear with full sets of the new metal-shafted clubs, only to be beaten by the woods.

At the time of his marriage in 1903, Patrick was living at 17 Fitzjohn's Avenue, Hampstead, London. But, before his marriage to Mabel Despard, an indenture was drawn up between the pair - a kind of prenuptial arrangement. Mabel brought more to the table than Pat, with shares in the Natal Bank, Preference Shares with DTW Murray Ltd., Ordinary Shares in the India Rubber & Gutta Percha Co. Ltd., and also shares in the National Discount Co. Pat had a 200 pound Life Assurance policy with the Clinical Medical & General Assurance Co., and a 1000 pound Life Assurance policy with the Scottish Provident Society.

I remember Pat from a couple of meetings. Once, when I was about seven he came up to stay with us in Glasgow. On this trip he brought along a leather strap (a tawse) which he gave to my father to be used on me if I got out of line. Not such an auspicious beginning, I thought. I particularly remember him taking cold baths in the mornings. He would jump in the bath and then lie down so that he could piston his legs back and forth to swoosh the water over him. This was accompanied by a loud trumpeting noise that went on for quite a while. Of course, much of the water was on the bathroom floor by the time he had finished. My poor mother had to hurry in, after he had gone, in order to mop up the flood. He also refused to have porridge with anything else, but salt. His efforts to convince me that this was the only way to eat the delicacy, went unrewarded.

Figure 16. Patrick Robertson in his soccer playing days with the London Scottish Club (c 1897).

The next time that I saw him was when I was in London on my way back from Denmark after a Boy Scout camp. I must have been about 14. I knew that my grandfather now lived on Well Road in Hampstead, and I convinced my scout leader that I was expected, and would be back in time for the night train north from Euston Station. I hopped a taxi to Pat's house. His housekeeper eyed me suspiciously as I stood at the door with my grubby Boy Scout uniform, decked out with kilt (Robertson hunting tartan, of course) and somewhat disheveled appearance from a week or so of roughing it in Denmark. After I explained who I was I was ushered upstairs to Pat's room. He was sitting in front of a gas fire in his nightie, and did not look well. Pat eyed me for a moment and it was then that I received my validation as he exclaimed "Yes, you're a Robertson alright."

He was interested in my activities but faded in and out during our conversation. However, he decided at one point that I needed some whisky and one of his Churchill cigars. He told me where to find the goods, but excused himself from participating. I think he just wanted to savor the moment of watching someone drink a single malt and smell the aroma of a cigar. Well, I obliged having touched neither whisky nor a cigar before, but nevertheless felt up to the task. As I was sitting there with whisky and cigar in hand, in walked the housekeeper who was visible nauseated by the sight. She announced that she was going to call my Aunt Aileen and rushed off downstairs. I could hear a raised voice on the phone and knew that trouble would soon be on the way. I managed to make my excuses and escaped before my aunt arrived. By the time I got home Aileen had called Dad about my behavior, but instead of being punished, Dad thought it was a good joke and laughed about the episode. Pat died about a year later.

June Robertson (1928) described Pat as "bit of a lad." She reports that on meeting Mary Wills, prospective wife of his brother Ronald, for the first time, he was heard to say "Well you are a damn lucky woman to be marrying a Robertson." Pat had a reputation for saying whatever came into his head and had no qualms about telling people exactly what he thought. My father, Douglas, reported that if he happened to be waking in Hampstead and spied his father Pat, on the same road, he would duck down an ally to escape having to walk with him. Apparently, the chances of Pat having an unpleasant encounter with someone that he decided needed a good talking to, was very strong.

At Pat's funeral the address stated that Pat loved all children and animals and was a pillar of society. To which his brother Ronald, asked in an audible whisper (which echoed around the church), "Who on earth wrote that drivel?"

At the graveside, all the attendants were asked to share the ropes that would lower Pat's coffin into the ground. But, the coffin got stuck because the hole was too small. All the attendants then jiggled the ropes trying to bounce Pat's coffin to its resting place. In exasperation, Douglas Robertson was heard to say, "One more minute and I'll jump on it."

At the time of his death Pat's estate was worth about 20,000 pounds and was shared between his son Douglas and daughter Aileen.

MABEL WILHELMINA DESPARD, Pat's wife, had a family residence originally in Ireland at Lacca Manor, Mountrath, as mentioned in the legal document drawn up prior to her marriage to Patrick. At the time of her marriage in 1903, Mabel was living at 3 Akenside Road, Hampstead, London, just a few hundred yards from the then Robertson household on Fitzjohn's Avenue in Hampstead.

Mabel was the 12th child of William Frederick Despard who was a Major in the 3rd Volunteer Battalion of the Queen's Own Royal West Kent Regiment. He liked shooting and was a contestant for the Queen's Prize in 1887. He was later the subject for a painting, commemorating the event, by Sir Robert Ponsonby Staples called "The Last Shot for the Queen's Prize." The competition was held on Wimbledon Common, in London, that year, but in 1890 the event was moved to Bisley, where the competition is still held today. William was about 60 at the time of the contest and, the Prince of Wales, the future Edward V11, also attended the event. William came from a very old aristocratic family that was descended from Count Phillip Despard, a Huguenot, who escaped France just after the St.

Bartholomew's Day massacre, in the 16th century. Thousands of French Protestants were killed by French Catholics during this time. Phillip received a commission from Elizabeth 1st as an administrator in Ireland (really a tax collector). Phillip's descendants who lived in Ireland created several different estates there.

Mabel had several interesting relations including an aunt Charlotte Despard who was an ardent suffragist and was imprisoned several times for her "non-violent" civil disobedience. She started the Women's Freedom League after she fell out with the Pankhurst sisters. She met Ghandi in London in 1909, who probably influenced her pacifist leanings toward WW1. That did not go down well with her brother Sir John French, Commander of the British Expeditionary Force in Europe, and later Lord Lieutenant of Ireland in 1918, commanding the "Black and Tans" during the Irish troubles. It was widely rumored that Charlotte also managed to obtain British military information, by peeking through her brother's military papers, and then sharing the information with her Irish friends. The other Despards' were not amused.

Later, Charlotte joined Maude Gonne, wife of the former IRA (Irish Republican Army) leader John McBride, who was hanged by the British, to protest conditions in Ireland. During that time Charlotte also joined Sinn Fein and the Communist Party. The following quote from Charlotte aptly summarizes her views "I have always believed in discontent - not grumbling, which is usually selfish and individual - but a disinclination to sit down idly, knowing things are wrong."

Another of Mabel's ancestors, Marcus Despard, was tried for treason in 1803 for his unfortunate association with Irish discontents, who were said to be plotting against the Crown. Marcus has the distinction of having been the last person in England to be "drawn on a bier" (a kind of board pulled by a horse) to the scaffold and then summarily hung, brought down and decapitated. The sensibilities of the times at least prohibited his body from being quartered and the pieces sent to other parts of the kingdom for public display, as a warning. It may have been a case of Marcus being in the wrong place, with the wrong people at the wrong time. Both Charlotte and Marcus were the subjects of recent books.

Not much is known about Mabel. As her portrait suggests she was something of a rare beauty with, perhaps, a delicate framework. Her name appears on the *1901 census* as a patient at Fitzroy Square Home Hospital, in South St. Pancras, London. Why she was there is not known but we can eliminate "epilepsy, lunacy, infectious diseases, contagious diseases, and midwifery cases," as these were not eligible conditions for entry into this well-to-do hospital. She seems to have been a good mother, notwithstanding her father's two marriages and probable short-term separation from his second wife, Mary Despard, when Mabel was quite young. Life with Patrick must have been demanding and Mabel died at the relatively young age of 54.

Figure 17. Mabel Wilhelmina Despard (c 1891).

AILEEN ROBERTSON, Pat and Mabel's second child, was born about 1910 and died about 1984 in Hampstead, London.

Aileen was a very beautiful young woman, inheriting her mother's good looks. Unfortunately, along with her good looks came a violent temper that sent most of her suitors packing. If her temper did not seal her fate with her admirers, then her father Patrick's short fuse and outspoken nature, did. She remained a spinster all her life. She trained as a teacher, but I am not sure how well she did in that profession. For years she volunteered at the Lawn Tennis Club in Wimbledon and was a staff member there during the championship seasons. One year, in the early 60s she went around all the players to collect autographs for me. People like Rod Laver, Margaret Smith, Maria Bueno, and Fred Perry, plus many more signed for her on The Queen's Club, West Kensington stationary. I still have them. Although tennis was not a game that I could master, I could see and appreciate the athletic part of the sport, and Aileen's effort on my behalf.

Aileen's interactions with the Robertson's of the north, particularly with her brother Douglas were testy at best. It seemed that things were said or not said, particularly over the phone, that give rise to offence and there would be silence for months or even years. Face to face, Aileen could not have been nicer and these times were worth remembering. She once took me on to Hampstead Heath to show me the memorial seat to Pat. Actually, it was a wooden bench, that she had erected on the Heath from which, on a clear day, there was a panoramic view over the heath. She actually made me get down on all fours, to look underneath and inspect, with her, the carvings that some of the local kids, "hooligans" she called them, had made with their pen knives. This happened when the seat was occupied by three snickering teenagers. In 1964 she also took me to see "It's a Mad, Mad, Mad, Mad World" (I may have forgotten a couple of "mads" in the title) in Leicester Square. I still remember Jimmy Durante, Mickey Rooney, Terry Thomas, Cid Caesar, and others. Unfortunately, these times were few and I when I moved to the USA I was out of favor. I tried several times, by mail, to encourage Aileen to send me information about the family, but she remained silent and eventually I received, through the mail, a returned envelope with the word "deceased" stamped over her address.

MARION ROBERTSON was the third child of James and Mabel Robertson. She was born in 1915 and died a few years later. Mabel was 43 at the time of Marion's birth.

RONALD DOUGLAS ROBERTSON (6G), was the fifth child of James and Margaret Robertson. He was born June 29, 1883 in Hampstead, London, and died February 8, 1968 in The Firs, Staplecross, Robertsbridge, Sussex, England. He married MARY (MOLLY) WILLS June 1917, daughter of Dr. S.J. Wills. She was born March 9, 1889 in Bexhill, Sussex, and died December 23, 1963 in Staplecross, East Sussex, England.

Ronald and Molly had two children MARGARET PEARCE born 1918 and JAMES PEARCE born 1920.

Life and times of RONALD DOUGLAS ROBERTSON:

While at school, at Highgate in Hampstead, Ronald played 1st XI cricket (1989, 1899, 1900, 1901) and was team Captain in 1902. He played 1st X1 soccer (1898, 1899, 1900) and was team Captain in 1901. He played Eton Fives in 1901 and 1902. In his post school days he played for London Caledonian Football Club (soccer) that won the London Charity Cup two years running. He had appearances for Middlesex and London, and played one match for Chelsea as an amateur.

He joined London Scottish Rugby Club in 1907, played two years in the "A" XV. From 1909 played regularly for 1st XV until WW1. He was selected for international Rugby Football in 1912 (Scotland versus France) and was team Captain for London-Scottish 1st XV rugby. He was also selected for London versus South Africa. He played cricket for Hampstead and Middlesex Young Amateurs versus Middlesex Young Professionals. Later, he played golf for Hertfordshire with a handicap of +1. After WW1 his handicap was +2. A remarkable feat considering that he had lost a leg and the sight of one eye in the war!

When Ronald was asked about his great sporting career, by his son Jimmy, Ronald said "In my opinion, any man who has the fortune to be born with an eye for ball games can make a show at any of them."

When war broke out Ronald immediately headed north to Aberdeen to enlist in the Gordon Highlanders. On September 1, 1914 when he joined the Gordon Highlanders his service # was 3398 and he identified himself as a non-conformist and 29 years of age. His measured vital statistics were height of 6'1" and weight of 190 pounds. He was given the rank of private. On September 9th he was promoted to Sergeant, and on the 22nd he was commissioned as a 1st Lieutenant in the 8th Battalion the Gordon Highlanders. Later, he was commissioned as a Captain on October 14, 1914, and assigned to the 9th Battalion the Gordon Highlanders (The Pioneers) under the command of Lt. Colonel H. Gordon.

On July 7, 1916 Ronald left for France with his Battalion. On 4th. January, 1916 he and the Battalion were in Lapugnoy and Flechin training. On the 15th the Battalion marched to Mazingarbe and began digging trenches. On the 23rd enemy sniper fire increased and the German Airforce was reported to be more active. On the 30th the enemy was very active with rifle grenades and at 1:15 a.m. the enemy ranged the new trench that was under construction. It was then that Ronald was wounded along with five other ranks. Ten days later Ronald had his right leg amputated below the knee and suffered a traumatic cataract to his right eye essentially blinding him on that side. Initially, he had been listed, mistakenly, as having been killed in action.

Figure 18. Scottish Rugby Team Vs. France (1912) – Inverleith, Edinburgh. Ronald Robertson back row, far left. Scotland won the match 31 points to 3.

Figure 19. Ronald Robertson in his Gordon Highlanders uniform (c 1914).

On April 8, 1916 Ronald embarked at Rouen for Southampton in England. Ronald was granted sick leave from April 8 to November 24, 1916, but was to be reassigned to the 11th Reserve Battalion of the Gordon Highlanders when medically fit. On December 2, 1916 Ronald had to undergo another operation to correct a protruding bone on his amputated right leg. By July 24, 1917 Ronald was passed fit for Officer's work and was assigned to HQ Command in Pall Mall, London. But, at the request of his employer, Thames Coal Company, Ronald applied for discharge from the army, which was granted on December 23, 1917.

The enormities of the sacrifices made in The Great War, and subsequent wars, are remembered each November 11 on Armistice Day in Britain – Veterans Day in the US. In his piece *The Fallen Flower of Scotland Remembered, The Daily Telegraph, November 11,*

78

2010, Brendan Gallagher paid special tribute to the sacrifices made by club members of the London Scottish rugby teams. Gallagher reported that 45 of 60 players in the four teams the club fielded on the last match of the season prior to the opening of hostilities, perished. In a rare photograph of the London Scottish rugby team that played United Services in 1914, and which included Ronald Robertson, eight players were listed as killed in action, four wounded, two severely wounded (including Ronald) and only one remained unscathed at the end of the war.

Following his discharge Ronald lived at 6 Grosvenor Place, SW and then in 1918 at 34 Platts Lane, Finchley Road, NW. Ronald was a junior partner and secretary for the Thames Coal Company at 34 Great Tower Street, London E.C. The building that Ronald worked in for Thames Coal was an historical landmark. His office was reputed to have a secret panel and passageway that was used by Nell Gwyn, the London actress, and a one time orange-seller and also paramour of Charles 11.

Figure 20. Ronald Robertson at work in his office at Great Tower Street, London (c 1936).

The company was involved with the manufacturer of munitions and steel/iron products for the war effort. Ronald's remuneration was largely dependent on what new business he was able to bring in from Gas Companies around the country. In this he became limited because of his war injuries which prohibited him from driving, and he had to rely more on his military pension of 100.00 pounds sterling per year, and seven shillings per day retirement benefit. Occasionally, some special opportunities would arise as during the General Strike when Ronald was appointed a Special Constable.

In 1921, Ronald moved with his wife Mary Wills and his children to Bankhorn, Meadway, Berkhampstead, Hertfordshire. The house was situated near a golf course and horse riding facilities. The move was partly at the insistence of Mary who wanted to put some distance between her and her meddling sisters-in-law.

In 1949 there was yet another move. Ronald and his brother-in-law Colonel Jack Wills bought The Grange in Staplecross, Robertsbridge, Sussex. Ronald busied himself with village activities in Staplecross. He joined the Ewhurst Parish Council and eventually became Chairman. In the early 1950s the Parish was beset with sewerage and fresh water problems and Ronald put his considerable talents to work in resolving many of these related problems. He is credited with having secured the fresh water supply for the village ending the dependency on the village well. Ronald also supported the village Youth Club, the village football team, the cricket club, and the British Legion. He was also a religious man and much involved with the village church. He, Mrs. Robertson, and Colonel Wills presented St. Mark's Church in Staplecross with an Alms Dish that is still in use today.

After Ronald's father, James, moved south from Edinburgh, the family shifted their religious affiliations from the Presbyterian Church to the Church of England. Certainly this was true for Ronald and it may have been true for his brother Pat. Douglas Robertson, Pat's son, was an Episcopalian all his life.

Ronald and his sister Elsie also provided support for the Hepburn Starey Blind Aid Society. Ronald and Mrs. Robertson would open their house, The Grange, to the old age pensioners serving luncheons and teas. Ronald would entertain the guests with rousing renditions of Harry Lauder favorites.

Although Ronald suffered significant wounds in WW1, and Colonel Wills suffered from a "stiff" leg as a result of an accident playing Polo in China, both set about to cultivate the lands around their home. This enterprise was likely financed with cash from a large legacy from Ronald's sister Elsie. Blackcurrant bushes were planted but the enterprise was not successful and, in 1966, most of the agricultural land was sold off leaving the house, an orchard, paddock, and a small wood comprising about three acres. Colonel Wills died in 1967 and Ronald died in the following year and the property was sold.

At Ronald's funeral there were significant tributes by Sir John Campbell, Vice President of the Hepburn Starey Blind Aid Society, and the address given by Reverend Kenneth Pearson, Rector of Ewhurst. The following extracts speak volumes for Ronald.

From Sir John J. Campbell, a Vice-President of the Society.
"In company with other members of the Society I was privileged to attend the Funeral Service of our much loved Chairman, Captain Ronald Douglas Robertson, on 12th February, 1968. A large concourse of mourners from all walks of life assembled in the Parish Church at Ewhurst to pay their last tribute to a great gentleman. The cortege was preceded by the Standard of the British Legion, signifying the close interest which, as an ex-service man, Captain Robertson took in that worthy organization. A most sincere and moving tribute, printed below, was paid by the Rev. Kenneth A. Pearson, Rector of Ewhurst, and it seemed to me appropriate that we should take leave of our dear friend in the friendly atmosphere of this small village church. I am sure this was as Ronald wished it."

Address given at the funeral service of RONALD DOUGLAS ROBERTSON in Ewhurst church, Sussex, on Monday, 12th February, 1968, by the Rev. Kenneth A. Pearson, Rector of Ewhurst.

"This is our last tribute of respect for a great man, strong in physique, strong in character like his native granite, strong in opinion, strong in action; always to borrow sporting metaphors, with his eye on the ball, going for the bowling, and playing fair.

Ronald was a superlative, all-round sportsman; excelling in his younger days in athletics, football (soccer and rugger) cricket, golf and tennis.

The 1914 War drew him into the Gordon Highlanders. There he was in his element, and his qualities of initiative and courage had full scope. He devoted to the welfare of the men under his command a fatherly understanding, brushing through red tape if need be. He was developing the qualities of a great soldier and would surely have risen high in command when wounds cut the career short. Deprived of a leg and of an eye he returned to civilian life.

Even so handicapped he was unbowed. There is a higher sort of courage than the instinctive reaction in time of danger: it is fortitude, the patient endurance of adversity and active triumph over it. Ronald had fortitude. He made light of his disabilities, ignored the pain, and with the help of an artificial limb continued to play golf and tennis with the best. He applied himself to business with determination and integrity.

Within the rugged frame beat a warm heart. Old comrades in arms found him a friend-in-need. The Hepburn Starey Blind Aid Society was a very special interest to which he gave generously of himself and of his means. Another was Major Carr-Gomme's Society (Abbeyfield) for providing suitable housing accommodation for old people. Some of us will remember those happy gatherings of old people from these homes, invited to spend a summer day at The Grange.

One secret Ronald kept from the world—his simple religious faith. He prayed; he read his bible; he came to church to receive Holy Communion. Never shall I forget the wonderful humility and fortitude of the old man, hardly able to walk, coming to the alter rails and kneeling there—yes, kneeling—and holding out his hands for the Bread of life.

Daily he read from a little book called Daily Light. One day he didn't read—the day he died. On that day the words were these:

'I am now ready to be offered, and the time of my departure is at hand. I have fought a good fight, I have finished my course, I have kept the Faith: henceforth there is laid up for me a crown of righteousness, which the Lord, the righteous Judge, shall give me at that day.'

With this passage from beyond the veil we leave him in trust and gratitude.

Dear Ronald: so frightening sometimes, so massive in single-minded drive forward, and so lovable. You have made an impress for good which some of us will never forget. You would have wished to go out with a cheerful flourish of trumpets. It could not be here, but *so* you have been met and welcomed on the other side. Rest in peace."

While I was looking through the documents about Ronald's life, I found it strange that on two occasions confusion arose with Ronald's name. The first occasion was with his war record and the other with his international rugby record. In both instances the name of Robert Dalrymple Robertson appeared. Robert was also a Captain in the Gordon Highlanders at the same time as Ronald although in a different battalion and in a different theater of operations. The name of Robert Dalrymple Robertson also appeared on the players' rugby profile distributed through the *Scottish Rugby Union* for the Scottish team that played against France in 1912. These errors have been corrected.

MARY (or Molly) WILLS , Ronald's wife, is described, by June Robertson (1928) as generous and beautiful. She was well read and intelligent, but seemed to like to control her family through emotional blackmail. She is credited with steering her brother Jack away from any marriage hopes and not providing much positive guidance to her daughter in matters of the heart. She had courage, and as a young woman she loved horse riding and hunting. She followed the Bexhill Harriers and once, single handedly, whipped a dog pack off a railway line to avoid an oncoming train. During WW1 she was a nurse and met Ronald while he was recuperating from his war wounds. Her brother Jack was apparently in the same ward but it is not clear what wounds he sustained, if any.

Jack Wills, Molly's brother, was initially in the Royal Artillery and then joined the Royal Army Service Corps (RASC) due to a leg injury while playing Polo. Jack retired from the army with the rank of Colonel and was awarded the Military Cross. His nickname was "Nunky" and June Robertson described him as "A soldier, a poet and a selfless saint, with a marvelous sense of fun." He was to live with Ronald and Mary Robertson in The Grange in Staplecross from 1949 until his death in 1967.

MARGARET ELIZABETH PEARCE ROBERTSON, Ronald's first child was born in 1918, in Hampstead, London; died 1992, in Wilmington, Sussex.

Margaret was known as "beetle" and was considered to be very good looking. Part of her education was at St. Andrew's University in Scotland, where she received a half Blue in fencing. She was a WAAF (Women's Auxiliary Air Force) during WW2 and developed tuberculosis soon afterward probably due to the conditions that she worked in. She studied to be a probation officer, and Jimmy, her brother, always claimed that she treated him as homework. June, her sister-in-law felt that she lacked a good sense of humour. Horses and cats received her main affection and she never married. In the mid 50s she moved from Staplecross to Willmington. Her ambitions for her horses far exceeded her means. The dressage competitions and shows required capital that she did not have. Rows could erupt quickly and could be followed by extended periods of isolation. Margaret, apparently, had many exchanges with Aileen, her cousin, both having similar dispositions. June reports that the lines of communication were never entirely cut and when Margaret developed stomach cancer, for the second time, she and Jimmy were with her in intensive care until eventually, after a heart attack, the life support systems were turned off. Her funeral was filled with family and friends, Jimmy chose "All Things Bright and Beautiful" as a dedication with the verse "forgive our foolish ways" which June thought most appropriate.

JAMES PEARCE ROBERTSON (7G) was born July 7, 1920, Hampstead, London; and died April 28, 2000, Andover, Hampshire. He married JUNE O'CARROLL SCOTT

James was affectionately known as" Jimmy." As a youngster his mother managed to get him into the prestigious St. Ronan's Preparatory School. In 1938, Jimmy was admitted to Saint Andrew's University on a non-degree program with the expectation of transferring to Cambridge. However, WW2 halted those plans. He served initially in Egypt in 1939 but contracted polio from which he recovered. Following parachute training he joined the Guards armored division in Normandy, and then posted to the 55th West Somerset Yeomanry Field Regiment R.A. (Royal Artillery). His unit moved

Figure 21. Margaret, Ronald, Mary (Wills), and Jimmy Robertson, Staplecross, Sussex, England (c 1955).

across Belgium and then on to Brussels. Then, supported the 1st British Airborne division at Arnhem where he was wounded. He was with British forces when German forces surrendered in Stavanger, Scandinavia. He would have moved on to Burma but the Japanese obligingly surrendered before he was committed. Jimmy continued to serve in the Army until 1964, when he retired with the rank of Major.

Jimmy had benefited from a legacy from his aunt Elsie, and being a "cash only" man, had indulged himself by spending some of it on hunting and polo. Enough remained to set up home with his wife June near Andover in southern England. At that time he and June took up the teaching profession. This was something of a match of convenience as a marriage grant was available for spouses doing teacher training together. However, both Jimmy and June were to find this a most rewarding occupation. During their 42 years of marriage, Jimmy had the unenviable task of arranging seven family funerals and disposing of five family homes. After the funeral of Jimmy's father in 1968, Jimmy ceremoniously built a bonfire and incinerated Ronald's artificial leg. A kind of Viking salute. Unfortunately, Jimmy experienced post polio symptoms in his early 70s and was laid low. June was able to nurse him at their home in Rose Cottage until he passed on.

JUNE O'CARROLL SCOTT, Jimmy's wife, was born in 1928 in Hereford.

June comes from an interesting family that has strong Irish roots. Among her famous ancestors is her great, great, grandfather Sir William Parker Carrol, who acquitted himself with great distinction during the Peninsula War (1811-1814) against Napoleon. Sir William fought against the famous French commander Marshal Ney, and whipped Joseph Bonaparte (Napoleon's brother) at Vittoria (1814), capturing Joseph's baggage train. This is a serving soldier's dream, for a baggage train, particularly one belonging to a "king," contains lots of booty. Much treasure found its way into English pockets, including those of Sir William. Many family heirlooms, from that period, are now on display at the *Limerick Civic Trust* in Pery Square Limerick, Ireland. Pictures, swords, medals are displayed there. Eventually, June intends to send many fine pieces of the Carrol family furniture for display at the museum.

June's father Tony O'Carroll Scott, was a professional soldier. Early in 1936 he was posted to India with his wife. June remained at home and was brought up, in her formative years, by her grandparents in Hereford. June was an only child and quickly learnt, at an early age, how to occupy her time in a positive way. She remembers the

86

pettiness of little girls during her first experiences of school, and having to adjust to other children. During the war years the skies were filled with barrage balloons. The wailing of air raid sirens often permeated the airways warning of the arrival of Nazi bombers. All too frequently there was a nightly glow, on the southern horizon. London was burning during the blitz.

In 1946 June landed a job with Norman Hartnell in the world of haute couture. She worked in the less glamorous workroom learning to sew and make "creations" for the very well to do. She had occasional sorties into the showroom to work with the models. Later, when her father became a Major General, June accompanied him to Hamburg, Germany and then to Singapore, where she learnt typing and shorthand and became secretary to Robin Woods, Archdeacon of Singapore. Her talents were then required in the service of Aileen Slim, wife of the Governor General, Field Marshal Sir William Slim, in Canberra, Australia. June was personal assistant and lady-in-waiting to Lady Slim. She remembers vividly the preparations for the visit of the young Queen Elizabeth 11 and the Duke of Edinburgh, and the huge impression that the beautiful Queen made on her.

On her return to England she worked as a floral decorator to Constance Spry and often made arrangements for #10 and #11 Downing Street (homes of the Prime Minister and Chancellor of the Exchequer of England).

Figure 22. June Robertson and Vicky (c 1990). A portrait of her ancestor, Sir William Parker, hangs to her left.

June met Jimmy Robertson through her Godfather Colonel Jack Wills, brother-in-law to Jimmy's father Ronald. After her marriage to Jimmy, June was an Army wife for seven years and traveled at home and abroad. When Jimmy retired from the army, both were to find a vocation in teaching. As a teacher, June was to find great pleasure although she despised the educational system of the 60s as she states "The educationalists of the sixties seemed hell-bent on destroying all the tried and trusted aims and skills of education, and replacing them with an ill conceived new crop of modern ideas which were to produce many problems in the years that followed. Service and sacrifice and duty were to be exchanged for self-expression, and not surprisingly, self interest; . . . they disregarded essential elements like discipline and thoughtful manners, . . ."

In 1994, June had her first book published "A Long Way from Tipperary," about her Irish roots, and then in 2005 she published her autobiography "Only Remember the Laughter."

CHAPTER 9

DOUGLAS ROBERTSON (7G), was born March 9, 1904 in Hampstead, London, and died December 9, 1977 in Glasgow, Scotland. He married LAURA ELIZABETH TALBOT-SMITH June 17, 1939 in All Saints Church, Glasgow, Scotland. She was born May 11, 1912 in Yokohama, Japan, and died October 29, 1994 in Stirling, Scotland.

Douglas and Laura had two children <u>LOARN DESPARD</u> born 1945, and ROSEMARY STRUAN born 1951. Loarn was to carry the family name forwards.

LIFE AND TIMES OF DOUGLAS ROBERTSON.

Douglas had a difficult time with his autocratic father, Patrick. His mother, Mabel, of whom he was very fond, called him "Pip," and she probably had great expectations of him. He attended Highgate School, in Hampstead, like his father and his uncle Ronald (1883) before him. He was a good athlete winning many sprints and hurdle events at school, but could never beat his great rival D.G.A. Lowe who won the 800 yds. race in the 1924 and 1928 Olympic Games.

Figure 23. Douglas Robertson high hurdling at Highgate School, London (c 1920).

After Highgate School, he wanted to go to university to study divinity, but Patrick had other ideas. Instead, he sent him north to Glasgow, to start work as a Civil Engineer in the Dalmarnock Iron Works of Sir William Arrol and Company. With the death of Sir William Arrol, Patrick probably figured that Arrols would become the family business, since his sister Elsie was wife of the late Sir William, and that Douglas would one day make it into the Board Room. But, that was not to be as Arrol's was eventually sold to new management and Douglas was stuck in a mid level management position with little hope of rising further.

However, Douglas did manage to enter the Episcopalian church as a Diocesan Lay Reader. He ran the local Sunday School at All Saint's Church in Jordanhill near our home in Anniesland, Glasgow. He was a very good mathematician, a facility that never passed down to me, and used to attend to the accounting needs of a large number of family members. Although, I did not know it he was also very good at classical languages, particularly Greek, and used to help the University of Glasgow with Old Testament Greek translations. For this work, he was later, to receive an honorary degree - A.Th. (Associate of Theology) from the University of Glasgow. Although he shrugged this event off, I think it meant a lot to him in coming close to his youthful goal of being an ordained minister.

Douglas was also very knowledgeable about current events and was invited, several times, to participate on the "Brains Trust," a radio show about local and national events. He was an arch conservative particularly when it came down to his clothes. He seemed unwilling to change with the times, and would not wear new-fangled shirts without pin down collars, and disliked belted trousers and waistcoats that were cut too close for comfort. Instead, he had many of his clothes made by a manufacturer in Ireland. He enjoyed monologues regarding his school days and stories about his father, but shared little else about other family members. Part of the problem may have been that because of his father's behavior, others of his near relations tended to avoid close contact. As a youngster, he did receive cards and letters form his aunts on their travels, but otherwise his mother seems to have been his main supporter until her untimely death when Douglas was about 22.

Figure 24. Douglas Robertson, second from left, participating in the BBC radio program The Brains Trust (c 1960).

LAURA ELIZABETH TALBOT-SMITH, Douglas's wife, was the youngest of four siblings with two older sisters and an older brother. She was called "Betty," and was born in Yokahama, Japan while her father, Richard Talbot, was there on the advice of his doctors. He had an ailing heart and was advised to work in a more temperate climate. Richard was an engineer and spent time in different parts of Japan helping Japanese companies build electrical generators to support their economy. But, the weather was not good and Richard tragically died of a heart attack, leaving his young wife Mary and four children almost penniless. Mary and her children sailed back to England and were eventually taken in by Richard's sister Laura who was a nursing sister at an outpatient facility in the Cowcaddens of Glasgow. Mary essentially became housekeeper for Laura in her home in Killearn, just north of Glasgow. Life was hard as

"Sister Laura," as she was called, was demanding and could be harsh but she provided shelter for the family and also education for each child.

Betty, like her sisters, became a nurse training at the Royal Infirmary in Glasgow. When she married Douglas she was quite young and WW2 was about to start. Glasgow suffered from the blitz and life was hard for most people, but when things got hard, then and later, Betty was uncomplaining. She had a marvelous sense of humor and, although she had a noticeable English accent, she could mimic Glasgow accents. She enjoyed comics like Stanley Baxter, one of Scotland's great comedians. She was very good at conversational French and enjoyed the visits of the French "onion" men who toured about Glasgow on their bicycles with strings of onions attached to the frames. The onions were sold door to door and she would speak French to them for a long time and the onion men were sure of a good sale at our house.

Betty would dearly have liked to travel more, but Douglas was not interested in that and all family excursions were restricted to local jaunts to Killearn, just north of Glasgow to see Betty's family, and to the Fife coast for the family summer holiday. After Douglas died, Betty managed to travel much more and visited friends and family in France, the south of England, the Persian Gulf, Holland, and the USA. Betty was a devoted mother who liked a good joke and people with character. When she died she requested that her ashes be spread over Ben Lomond. Dutifully her daughter, a nephew, a niece and I braved the slopes on a wet and cold day. We managed to get about three-quarters of the way to the top before rain, mists, and exhaustion (for some) forced a halt. Betty's ashes were cast over the slopes of Ben Lomond near a spot with a terrific view of the Loch, below. After our decent, we toasted Betty's memory with a single malt, or two, in the Ben Lomond Hotel.

Figure 25. Laura Elizabeth Talbot-Smith (c 1936).

ROSEMARY STRUAN ROBERTSON was born May 17, 1951, in Glasgow, Scotland. She married (1) LANDALE CRANFIELD in Glasgow, and they had one adopted daughter LAURA CRANFIELD born February 12, 1988. Laura attended Dollar Academy and was accepted at Dundee University to read history. Rosemary married (2) PETER LAWRY in August 2004 in Portree, Skye, Scotland.

Rosemary was educated at the Park School in Glasgow and then at Edinburgh University where she earned B.Sc. degree. She became a Social Worker joining her many forebears who followed a life of service to others. Although, I say it myself, I do think my sister is quite a cool person. Her accomplishments are not startling but they are, nevertheless, important. She has cultivated and maintained a wide circle of loyal friends. She built and developed a successful B&B beneath Castle Campbell in Dollar, and she raised an adopted daughter with love and determination.

I have only once seen her mortified. She was then about 10 and beginning to notice boys. It was during a family trip to Inchcailloch, the island on Loch Lomond, near Balmaha. We had rowed across in a dinghy for a picnic lunch on a beautiful day. After lunch my sister took a stroll along the beach. My father decided to take the dinghy for a row off the shoreline. As he passed Rosemary he happened to call out to her using his pet name for her. Unfortunately, a patrol of boy scouts was setting up camp nearby and were well within earshot. As I gazed at Rosemary I could see her face turning bright crimson and her pace quicken to a headlong run. Taking the example of my father, and in perfect unison, the scouts called out to Rosemary, "Wee, wee! Wee, wee!" My father continued to hear about that in no uncertain terms from my sister, for weeks to come.

Figure 26. Giving the bride away (Rosemary)
Portree, Isle of Skye (2004).

95

CHAPTER 10

LOARN DESPARD ROBERTSON (8G), was born June 3, 1945 in Glasgow, Scotland. He married ANNE MARLENE SCOTT July 14, 1978 in Champaign, Illinois. She was born June 27, 1956 in Ottawa, Illinois.

Loarn and Anne Robertson have four children RORY DUNCAN, born 1979, RACHAEL DESPARD, born 1982, KEEGAN JEAN, born 1985, and MAIRI ALEXANDRA, born 1989.

I (Loarn) was born on a Sunday at the Royal Infirmary in Glasgow. I first lived in a flat on Crow Road, Anniesland on the west side of Glasgow, and one of my first remembrances was the street lights coming on at night, and my patiently waiting for the nightly event. I also remember being pushed by my mother in a pram to exchange ration cards for goods. The cards were still required for many items in short supply, after WW2. When I was about six the family moved to Ancaster Drive, about a half mile away from the flat, into a three storey terrace house. I had a top floor room and that had a great view of the Campsie Hills, to the north, and the railway line that carried a large number of steam trains that wheezed and tooted throughout the day. On one side lived the family of a lawyer, and on the other a family of Plymouth Brethren. The sound of the harmonium and something less than choral unison could be heard through the walls on Sunday mornings and an occasional weekday celebration, featuring the Brethren.

The neighborhood was a mixture of the fairly well-to-do and the not so well endowed. Anniesland bordered two fairly tough neighborhoods, Clydebank and Temple. As I was growing up I fell in with one of the Anniesland gangs and experienced several pitched battles against gangs from Temple. Some of these encounters resulted in bloody noses, black eyes and bruises, but nothing worse. Most of the issues were over territorial rights and dare devil exploits. A favourite dare devil activity was to see how long you could stay in a tenement close (a three or four storey apartment building made of sandstone with tiled hallway floors and a long stairwell) after setting

96

off a 1d "banger" (exploding firework) during Guy Fawlks night. When the "banger" went off in the close, the noise was absolutely deafening, particularly if it was set off at the top of the stairwell, which was the biggest dare. The resulting racket used to bring the tenants running to see what was amiss. No heart attacks were recorded but it livened up the night.

My parents were not amused by many of his antics and I found myself with less free time and weekends taken up with trips to my Grandmother's house in Killearn, about 13 miles north of Glasgow. I can remember the intoxicating aroma of breakfast being made with bacon, sausage, black pudding, white pudding, tomatoes, onion and egg all being cooked up in the same skillet and the residue being mopped up with fried bread. Nothing was wasted and the taste was fantastic. Of course, that whole gastronomic delight would be severely frowned on in today's health conscious society. But, back then work soon followed the meal. In season, countless hours were spent pruning hedges, trees and other things in easy reach. I picked fruit in the spinney where my aunt grew alpine strawberries, raspberries, gooseberries, black and red currents, pears, and an assortment of vegetables and legumes. There was a twice annual canning session where things were jarred and stored in a back pantry for later consumption. It was an all-family event with no one excused. But, there were also distractions to the work, like jaunts down to Killearn glen. During the seasons, the glen was filled with bracken, bluebells felled trees and paths filled with a canopy of pine needles. There were waterfalls, still pools and running water and bogs in different parts of the glen. It was a great place for war games and hiking. I always marveled and how tough it was to try and walk through green bracken. I actually used to try and run through it with my sister and cousins and usually came a cropper, after being snared by the unyielding bracken shoots.

Close to his Grandmother's house was Drumbeg Loan, a steep road that led down from the Main Road, where my Grandmother's house was situated, to the old Station Road, below. It was great to bike down as long as your brakes were sound. But, you had to push the bike back up the Loan, as there was no chance of peddling up. At the bottom of the Loan was McGowan's Saw Mill where I occasionally worked. Really, I was just tolerated, but along the way learnt to use a long saw, make tea in "billy-cans," stack lumber and occasionally drive the "cran" - an old WW2 vehicle that was converted into a log lifting hoist. I was not much good at driving the "cran," but it gave the men a good laugh during lunch when I was allowed to try to drive the vehicle off road. I can still remember the smell of fresh cut wood and the resin that took ages to remove from my hands, after work.

On my jaunts up and down the Loan, I used to pass a thatched house, that belonged to an old geezer called B'iler (short for Boiler) Wilson. B'iler was a bachelor and lived on his own. He had made his personal fortune on Clydeside, in its heyday, by building and outfitting many ships with steam boilers. He probably engaged the huge Fairfield Cranes (biggest in the world at that time) that lined the Clyde dock areas to haul massive engineering pieces like ship's boilers. Incidentally it was Sir William Arrol's company that built these cranes.

B'iler was something of an eccentric. Around his home was a huge garden that he had transformed into an adventure playground. It was so well camouflaged that you could not tell immediately that it was there. I had heard about a huge oak with different launching stages from which you could climb up to, and then swing out from, using a high tethered rope. But, as was revealed later there was much more including trestles that had to be climbed vertically, with attached ladders, laid horizontally, that you could clamber across. The whole structure was covered in ivy. There were thickets with holes cut in different shapes so that you could crawl through and connect with metal tubing that led in all sorts of different directions. There were balance boards, pits and a maze made of hedgerow. This was a rough and ready creation, but was just the thing for youngsters. At the time, I did not know that B'iler was a bachelor and envied his children the use of the garden. Then one day, while pushing my bike up the Loan, I noticed some of the village lads playing in the garden. Curiosity got the best of me and asked what they were doing there and was told "J'ist ask the gaffer, if ye can play." Well I did. Nervously, I walked up to B'iler's front door and knocked. Presently, the old man came to the door and I asked if I could play. "Whit's the password?" asked the old man gruffly.

"Password? I don't know the password," I responded, apologetically. The old man hurried away and wrote something down on some paper. "Here," he said, "repeat this correctly and ye can play. Correctly, mind!" With that he closed the door.

The contents of the paper looked like gibberish, to me, and so I hurried back to my grandmother's house to ask for help. My grandmother seemed to know about B'iler and his password. I tried to say the words phonetically and got some help with the pronunciation. After a while I determined to try the password on old B'iler. Confidently, I knocked on his door. After a bit, B'iler appeared. "Well? He asked impatiently.
Loarn started "Timi dunna nae us.... fenti."
"No, no, lad. Practice some more." He shut the door and shuffled away.
Well there were several more trips to B'iler's front door, but each time the rendition of the password fell short and I was sent packing. At last, I felt that he had mastered the phrase. Back I marched and for the umpteenth time, it seemed, knocked on the door. Momentarily the old man appeared.
"Well lad, back again, eh? O.K. let's hear it."
"Timeo Danaos et donna fetrentes."
I thought that it sounded good but was not sure. B'iler had a twinkle in his eye as he said approvingly "Ye have the run o' the playground."

The Latin scholars among you will recognize the password as meaning *I fear the Greeks, even when bearing gifts* – the epitaph for the Trojans after their experience with a wooden horse made by the Greeks. It was my first exposure to Latin and I am not sure, if later, when Latin was introduced at school, that this experience convinced me to drop the subject, at the earliest opportunity.

Some years later B'iler died and his house was sold and the garden was closed to those who knew the password. After his passing B'iler left a small fortune to many needy charities that he had supported over his lifetime.

My first school in Glasgow was Miss Bishop's School in Kelvinside, off Great Western Road. Miss Bishop had a distinctive Dickensian look to her, dressed in dark habits, a permanent bun for her hair, steel rimmed glasses and gaunt features. I was petrified most of the time in that one room school. When he was six or so, I somehow managed to enter the Glasgow Academy as a student. Several Aitkin family members had been educated there. After a time, it became obvious that my academic talents were limited, and that I was unlikely to venture down the hallowed halls of Oxford or Cambridge, which had been my father's strong desire. Instead, in my later years, I was able to make some impression on the games field, playing for the Glasgow Academy first XV rugby team for several years, and then being chosen to represent the Scottish Schoolboys vs. English Schoolboys in Richmond, London in 1964. The "Auld Enemy" was routed that day. I also found that I could throw rocks a fair distance and managed to be selected for the Scottish Schools Athletic (track and field) Team as a shot putter for a couple of years.

Summer holidays were spent at Lundin Links on the Fife coast. Fife was my mother's favorite Scottish county. The family used to camp out at the Golf View hotel. Golf, swimming in the North Sea (for those that dared), and touring Fife were standing orders, weather permitting. In the summer evenings, family members would stroll down to Lower Largo, for ice cream and walk along the sea jetty. It was a relaxing place to be. Strangely enough, Lundin Links is only a few miles from Newburn parish where this story began.

Towards the end of my schooldays, and with some effort, I managed to gain several Ordinary level and Higher level exam certificates, enough at least to gain entry to Loughborough Colleges in Leicestershire, England. There I was to train as a teacher. My experiences at Loughborough were exhilarating. My academics improved and I made the Loughborough first team rugby XV in my first year. I just happened to luck out as a senior player, in my position, was injured, and I got the job. I was fortunate to play alongside some of the future best players in the UK, like David Rollitt (England), John Taylor (Wales and British Lions), Colin McFadyean (England and British Lions) and Gerald ('tiger') Davies (Wales and British Lions). Then there were the instructors like John Robins (Wales and British Lions) who coached rugby. He was a quiet, unassuming man with tremendous personal presence that instilled confidence and respect. There were others too, like Geoff Gowan (athletics) and Eric Blackadder (gymnastics) that impressed me greatly with their professionalism and personalities.

Following Loughborough, I moved further south to London and lived in Chelsea, just off the Fulham Road. My first teaching job was at William Penn School in Red Post Hill - a tough part of the east end of London, across the River Thames from the Fulham Road. Many of the kids there had very hard lives with broken families, abusive parents, and little hope of escape from the poverty that surrounded

Figure 27. Sports Day at Loughborough Colleges, 1966. From the left David Poole (hurdles,) the author (throws), John Knowles (sprints). All winners & personal best efforts.

them. Yet, many were the most genuine children that I was to meet. Many were hard-working, honest and responsible. Later, I moved to another job at Thames Valley Grammar School in Twickenham, very near the London Scottish rugby club that, as an exile Scot, I wanted to join. Teaching at Thames Valley was considerably easier than at William Penn. I lived in Richmond in a one room flat in a cull de sac. I dearly loved living there. From Richmond it was easy to get to most places around London, by underground. The rugby club was close by and Richmond was filled with curiosity shops and fabulous pubs that I enjoyed visiting.

It was while in London that I had my first experience of the US. I was invited to join a rugby tour of the east coast with London Scottish. Several other rugby clubs and individuals were on tour with London Scottish including some very drunk Australians that somehow had joined up with one of the touring clubs in London. On every encounter the "Aussies" seemed to be in a constant state of inebriation. I was very much impressed with the US and was even offered a job coaching Brandeis University rugby team in Boston. But, I still had dreams of appearing at Murrayfield, Edinburgh (home of Scottish rugby) wearing a Scottish rugby jersey with a number 1 on the back, and scoring the winning try to beat England in the Calcutta Cup match. However, that was not to be, for after returning home from the US, an injury put paid to any notion that he had about a trial for national honors on the rugby field.

Instead, I decided to focus on returning to the US to work on an advanced degree. With a little more cerebral perspiration I was able to pass entrance examinations to the University of Illinois in Champaign, Illinois. There I met and fell in love with Anne. After we both graduated we were married in Champaign, and then had various adventures living, working and playing in Downey, California; Portland, Oregon; Bakersfield California; Durham, New Hampshire; and Tuscola, Illinois.

Anne is the daughter of a former professor at the University of Illinois, John Scott, whose academic expertise was in agricultural economics. Fortunately, for me, his financial and business acumen was passed on to his daughter. Her wise decisions have kept the family afloat these many years. Anne's mother, Barbara was one of the first women to gain a Ph.D. degree in child psychology. Both she and her husband are from Midwest farming families and passed on the ethics of hard work and responsibility to their children. Anne, seems to be able to take on many different tasks at the same time and juggles family, work, education and social activities with great ease. Currently, she has just completed a Ph.D. program in Social Work while holding down a full time position at the College of Education at the University of Illinois.

Along the way, Rory, Rachael, Keegan and Mairi were born, and it is probably fitting that with their introduction this yarn should come to a close. First, a few brief comments. James Robertson (1872) is the only other male that might have married and produced heirs. But, you may remember that his name disappeared around 1900 in Cupar, Fife. If he did not survive, then, the four children above are the last of this branch of the Robertson clan possessing the legal name of Robertson.

All the girls have either attained or are working toward advanced degrees in the social services (social work and health). In this they emulate many of their forebears and their futures look bright. Keegan married Tony Aggers in 2009 and recently produced their first child Felicity Anne. Rory, may hold pride of place as the last male heir to this branch of the Robertson clan. Yet, as has been recounted the name and blood line continues through other family members and will continue through future marriages. In this we are still all connected.

END.

Figure 28. Anne and Loarn's wedding day, Champaign, Illinois (1978).

APPENDICES

Appendix A

Migrations of Family Heads of Households.

The following list shows the known migrations of different heads of families. In the list, a region within which family members were known to reside is identified. The first date represents the appearance of the family member in the region, and the second date, in parentheses, is a birth date of the family member, followed by a known location.

FIFE & ENVIRONS
1711 David Robertson (1690) – Moorehead, Newburn Parish
1722 David Robertson (1722) – Moorehead, Newburn Parish
1756 Peter Robertson (1756) – Craighead, Newburn Parish
1851 James Robertson (1798) – Bonnygate, Cupar
1856 James Robertson (1798) – 21 Bonnygate, Cupar
1871 Margaret Robertson (1807) – 19 Bonnygate, Cupar
1871 Andrew Robertson (1836) – 14 Bonnygate, Cupar
1876 Anne Robertson (1827) – 75 Bonnygate, Cupar
1881 Andrew Robertson (1836) – 21 Bonnygate, Cupar
1889 George Simpson (1860) – (Margaret Ireland Robertson) – Airth, Stirlingshire
1891 Janet (Thallon) Robertson (1938) – Westfield Park, Cupar
1953 Charles Wood (1874) - (Annie Hay Robertson) – Kirkaldy

MIDLOTHIAN
1861 Robert Wallace (1831) (Margaret Robertson) – Gayfield Square, Edinburgh
1871 James Robertson (1839) – Preston Terrace, Edinburgh
1881 James Robertson (1839) – Mayfield Terrace, Edinburgh
1901 Janet (Thallon) Robertson – Dalhousie Terrace, Edinburgh
1956 Margaret Ireland (Robertson) Simpson – Ladysmith Road, Edinburgh

LONDON & THE SOUTH

1881 Robert Wallace (1831) (Margaret Robertson) – Finborough Road, Kensington, London

1881 James Robertson (1839) – Houghton Lodge, Ellerdale Road, Hampstead, London

1889 Robert Wallace (1831) (Margaret Robertson) – Beaufort Street, Chelsea, London

1901 James Robertson (1839) – Fitzjohn's Avenue, Hampstead, London

1907 James Robertson (1839) – Chesterfield Gardens, Hampstead, London

1907 Patrick Robertson (1872) – Hillfield Road, Hampstead, London

1913 Patrick Robertson (1872) – Netherhall Gardens, Hampstead, London

1913 Maud and Elsie Robertson (1875, 1878) – Finchley Road, Hampstead, London

1921 Ronald Robertson (1883) – Berkhamsted, Herts.

1937 Aileen Robertson (1910) – Howitt Close, St. John's Wood, London

1949 Ronald Robertson (1883) – Staplecross, Sussex

1957 James Robertson (1920) – Penton Mewsey, Andover

1961 Patrick Robertson (1872) – Well Road, Hampstead, London

1968 Loarn Robertson (1945) – Fulham Road, Chelsea, London

GLASGOW AND ENVIRONS

1921 Hugh Aitken (1865) - (Eva Robertson) – Bearsden

1930 Douglas Robertson (1904) – Crow Road, Anniesland

USA

1971 Loarn Robertson (1945) – Champaign, Illinois

Appendix B

This appendix has to do with general information about the Robertson Clan, things Scottish and surnames of family members that were not originally Robertson's. By convention, the ladies who married took the name Robertson, while female Robertson offspring, who later married, took the names of their husbands. You will see however, that surnames and also Christian names are repeated throughout the generations. Surnames, are of course a fairly recent phenomenon, emerging over the last 1,000 years or so, particularly following the Norman Conquest. The revered Robert The Bruce, of "Braveheart" and Bannockburn fame, was of Norman descent. As the film showed there were multiple animosities among the early clans, and much jockeying for power particularly for the top spot of king. During the early wars for independence the Balliol and Bruce families were going at it head to head.

The Robertson clan is indeed an old one, predating the time of the Bruce by many centuries. William Skene the much respected historian of the 19th century wrote "the Robertsons of Struan are unquestionably the oldest family in Scotland, being the sole remaining branch of that royal House of Atholl which occupied the throne during the 11th and 12th centuries." The ancient district of Atholl, in central Scotland, was the location for many families having ties to the regality of the land. At one time clan Donnachaidh (Duncan), the forerunner to Clan Robertson, owned about half the lands of Atholl that became an earldom – that is an area inhabited by high ranking relatives to the ruling royal family. There were many Donnachaidh families in the area, perhaps as many as 25 branches, including the Robertsons of Struan, the Robertsons of Lude, the Robertsons of Faskally and the Robertsons of Auchleeks. Struan was eventually to become the family from which all the Robertson clan chiefs were to emerge. Other families settled in Atholl including some Stewarts, Butters, Spaldings, Smalls and Fergussons. When the Stewart dynasty of kings and queens emerged, the line of John Murray, whose mother was a high ranking Stewart, erected a dukedom in Atholl that continues to this day. The Murray family residence is Blair Castle, which has the distinction of being the last castle in Britain that was laid siege to.

On the front cover of this book is the image of an Atholl Highlander. The Atholl Highlanders are the only private army in Britain and Europe. During a visit to Blair Castle by Queen Victoria Her Majesty was much impressed by the Atholl Highlanders and the kind attention provided to Her by the sixth Duke of Atholl. As a gift, she presented the Duke with colors (in 1845), giving the Highlanders the right to bear arms. Today, the private army numbers about 45 persons and performs ceremonial duties. Membership is only by invitation of the Duke of Atholl, and some of the rank and file are former high ranking officers from the regular army. But, in years past the resident Duke of Atholl called up his Highlanders to fight during the Jacobite rebellions (1689, 1715 and 1745) against the English government. In 1746 at Culloden, the final battle between the Scots and English on British soil, Atholl Highlanders, that included representatives of Clan Robertson, supported the right flank of the Jacobite army. Prince Charles Edward Stewart, commander of the Jacobites on that day, stood nearby. A stone marker, commemorating the stand of the Atholl Highlanders can be found today on Culloden field.

Figure 29. A stone marker commemorating the stand of the Atholl Highlanders at Culloden Field.

As already mentioned the early name for the clan was not Robertson but "Donnachaidh" or Duncan. The first recognized clan chief was Donnachaidh Reamhar or "Stout Duncan." The stout part referred to his character and not his waistline. How the name Donnachaidh became Robertson has some legends about it. I like the one about Stout Duncan arriving late, with the Donnachaidh Clan at the battle of Bannockburn, in 1314, to support the Bruce. At the time the Bruce himself was under a severe attack by the English and at one point his position looked hopeless. Stout Duncan arrived in the nick of time to lay waste the English and save the Bruce. For this favor the Bruce, after the battle, bestowed the name "Sons of Robert" or Robertson onto the Donnachaidhs. A later version of the name change has the 4th Chief, Robert Riabhach Duncanson, hunting down the assassins of James 1st and handing them over to the Crown for summary trial and execution by hanging, drawing and quartering. Robert was rewarded with clan lands in what was called the feudal Barony of Struan, around present day Glen Garry and Rannoch Moor in central Scotland.

The Clan motto is "Virtutis Gloria Merces" or "Glory is the Reward of Valour." There are many symbols, in nature, supporting the Clan that relate to its history. The plant badges for the Clan are the bracken fern and fine leafed heath, common to Clan lands on the south side of Loch Rannoch. The Clan war cry is "Garg'n Uair Dhuisgear," Gaelic for "fierce when roused." The Chief's coat of arms consists of three silver wolf heads on a red shield, supported by a serpent and a dove. These supporters identify the origin of the Clan as being descendants of Saint Colomba since in Scots heraldry the dove signified descent from the Saint. And, the privy seal of Alexander 111, the last of the royal line of Atholl, contains the serpent and the dove supporters with the proverb "be wise as the serpent and gentle as the dove."

Well, the Robertsons like many clans were not that gentle. They were in fact quite small, in numbers, compared to some of their neighbors, and territorial fighting continued through the ages. That combined with some chiefs being less than good stewards of family holdings, slowly saw Robertson land eroding. However, throughout their early history the Robertson's remained faithful to the Royal Stewarts for over three centuries. Donald, the tutor of Struan, fought with Montrose for Charles 1 in 1644. The "Poet" Chief Alexander joined Bonnie Dundee at the Battle of Killiecrankie in 1689. He was pardoned by Anne 1 in 1703. But, then he came out again and fought in the Jacobite rebellions of 1715 and as an old man in 1745 with Charles Edward Stewart (Bonnie Prince Charlie). These losing causes were to signal the bitter loss of and occupation of Robertson lands. After the rebellion of 1715, the English General Wade built Rannoch Barracks, at the head of Loch Rannoch, to retain an English garrison on Robertson lands to keep an eye on them.

After the final defeat of the Highlanders at Culloden there emerged a period of unparalleled troubles for many Highlanders and Jacobite sympathisers. It also drove things traditionally Scottish underground. Clans were dismantled, clan lands were absorbed for sheep farming, the highland garb was outlawed, and the pipes were considered instruments of war. Many Scots were forced to leave their homeland. It was a low point for all Scots.

Years later, Sir Walter Scott began to write epic tales about this rebellious period in his Waverley novels. They caught the romantic imagination of the nation. Two additional events propelled things Scottish back into the public eye. One, was the discovery of the Scottish Regalia (crown, sceptre, and sword and scabbard) the symbols of Scottish Royal authority, that had been boarded up in the old Crown Room of Edinburgh Castle, after the Union with England in 1707. The second event was the Royal visit to Edinburgh in 1822. Sir Walter Scott had organized this in a hurry for the new King George 1V. This event was organized with tartan in mind. George was even persuaded to display his portly body in the Royal Stewart tartan. The ensemble, consisted of king's bonnet feathered as Chief of Chiefs together with a Highland Dirk, a Basket Hilt Highland sword of polished steel with hilt and mountings inlaid with gold. Pair of fine inlaid Highland pistols, together with Powder Horn with different colored Scottish gems were also displayed on his person. A great gold chain girded his frame, and shoes with gold rosettes and studied gems adorned his feet. All for about 1200 pounds Scots.

Balls, parades, feasts and theatre attended the King and he was enthralled. Although, the banning of wearing the kilt had been lifted earlier, it was the Royal visit and Scott's innovation that occasioned the renaissance of interest in Scottish culture. It remains very much in evidence, today.

The following is a list of surnames of females who married into the Robertson Clan, and of males who married Robertson women. These are presented alphabetically, and where appropriate, the clan associated with the name is given together with the clan motto. In other cases, where no associated clan could be found, the origin of the name is provided.

Surname Derivations, Clan Affiliations & Mottos.
Aitken – Clan Gordon (motto – "by courage not craft")
Allen – Clan MacFarlane (motto – "this I'll defend")
Arrol – Clan Hay (motto – "keep the yoke")
Bell – Clan Macmillan (motto – "I learn to succour the distressed")
Collie – Of local Aberdeenshire origin, possibly around the 13th century
Cranfield – Of English origin
Deer or Dire – Of Aberdeenshire origin, 14th century.
Despard – French Huguenot origin 13th century, meaning "of the sword"
Durlot – Of French origin.
Gallagher – Of Irish origin, Donegal
Ireland – Of Fife origin around 13th century
Jervise – Of Scottish origin 13th century, probably derived from a personal name
Judd – Of Scottish origin 14th century
Laird – Clan MacLean (motto – "virtue mine honour")
Lawry – Clan McLaren (motto – "the Boar's Rock"), spelling 17th century, possible meaning "foxy"
Leggat – May be originally an old English personal name, or a tribute meaning "an ambassador," name appears around Stirling in the 15th century

Lock – Clan Douglas (motto – "never behind")
McCallum – Clan Malcolm (motto – "God is my refuge")
McGregor – Clan McGregor (motto – "Royal is my race")
McVeigh – Clan MacDonald (motto – "by sea and by land")
Scott – Clan Scott (motto "I love")
Simpson – Clan Fraser (motto – "all my hope is in God")
Smith – Of English origin but also related to Clan Chattan (motto – "touch not the cat without a glove")
Stewart – Clan Stewart (motto – "courage grows strong at a wound")
Strathdee – Of local origin around Aberdeen, from the strath on the River Dee.
Thallon – Of Fife origin 16th century
Wallace – Clan Wallace (motto – "for Liberty")
Wills – Of English origin, but also related to Clan Gunn (motto – "either peace or war")

Appendix C

Occupations of Early Ancestors
Actor
Barrister (courtroom lawyer)
Constable (policeman)
Farm Labourer
Flesher (butcher)
Tanner
Bank Clerk
Excise (Customs) Man
Bank Inspector
Homemaker
Clergyman
Physician
Member of Parliament
Nurse
Solicitor (manager of legal cases, advocate in a lower court)
Engineer
Bridge Builder
Teacher
Social Worker
Soldier
Company Director
Hotelier
Newspaper Editor
University Professor

Appendix D

Kinship with David Robertson

The kin of David Robertson are presented alphabetically followed by the relationship.

Aggers, Anthony D. (husband of 6th great-granddaughter)
Aggers, Felicity Anne (7th great-granddaughter)
Aitken, Chloe Brianna Amber (7th great-granddaughter)
Aitken, Douglas (4th great-grandson)
Aitken, Douglas Willsoun (6th great-grandson)
Aitken, Fergus Shaun Wallace (6th great-grandson)
Aitken, Finlay, James Lewis (7th great-grandson)
Aitken, Garry Robertson (5th great-grandson)
Aitken, Hamish Willsoun (5th great-grandson)
Aitken, Hugh Wallace (husband of the 3rd great-granddaughter)
Aitken, Ian Malcolm (5th great-grandson)
Aitken, Iona Laird (5th great-granddaughter)
Aitken, Kenneth (4th great-grandson)
Aitken, Kenneth Malcolm Harold (6th great-grandson)
Aitken, Mairi Elaine Zoe (6th great-granddaughter)
Aitken, Malcolm (4th great-grandson)
Aitken, Philip Ruiriadh Braden (7th great-grandson)
Aitken, Robert Malcom (6th great-grandson)
Aitken, Ross Garry (6th great-grandson)
Aitken, Scott Gregor (6th great-grandson)
Aitken, Sophie Gemma (7th great-granddaughter)
Aitken, Steven Damian (6th great-grandson)
Aitken, Tristan Francis Ian (6th great-grandson)
Aitken, Wallace (4th great-grandson)
Allen, Carolyn Betty (Wife of the 5th great-grandson)
Arrol, William (Husband of the 3rd great-granddaughter)
Bell, Sophia (Wife of the grandson)
Collie, Robert John (Husband of the 3rd great-granddaughter)
Cranfield, Landale (Husband of the 5th great-granddaughter)
Cranfield, Laura (6th great-granddaughter)
Deer, Alexander (Father-in-law)
Deer, Suffia (Sophia) (Wife)

Despard, Mabel Wilhelmina (Wife of the 3rd great-grandson)
Durlot, Virginie (Wife of 6th great-grandson)
Gallagher, Elizabeth (Wife of the 6th great-grandson)
Gray, Alfred (Husband of the 3rd great-granddaughter)
Harvey, Jain (Mother-in-law)
Ireland, Margaret (Wife of the great-grandson)
Jervies, Isabel (Daughter-in-law)
Judd, Margorie Winifred (Wife of the 4th great-grandson)
Laird, Eilla Mabel (Wife of the 4th great-grandson)
Lawry, Peter (Husband of the 5th great-granddaughter)
Leggat, James Douglas (6th great-grandson)
Leggat, Joanna Rachel (6th great-granddaughter)
Leggat, John Brian (Husband of the 5th great-granddaughter)
Lock, Hazel F. (Wife of the 5th great-grandson)
McCallum, Fiona Elizabeth (Wife of the 6th great-grandson)
McGregor, Anne (Wife of the 5th great-grandson)
McVeagh, Margaret Elizabeth (Wife of the 2nd great-grandson)
Robertson, Agnes Sophia (3rd great-granddaughter)
Robertson, Aileen (4th great-granddaughter)
Robertson, Andrew (2nd great-grandson)
Robertson, Anne (2nd great-granddaughter)
Robertson, Annie Hay (3rd great-granddaughter)
Robertson, Catherine Taylor (2nd great-granddaughter)
Robertson, David (Son)
Robertson, David (Great-grandson)
Robertson, David (2nd great-grandson)
Robertson, David (Robbsone) (Self)
Robertson, Douglas (4th great-grandson)
Robertson, Elizabeth (Daughter)
Robertson, Elsie (3rd great-granddaughter)
Robertson, Isabel (Daughter)
Robertson, James (Grandson)
Robertson, James (Great-grandson)
Robertson, James (2nd great-grandson)
Robertson, James (3rd great-grandson)
Robertson, James Pearce (4th great-grandson)
Robertson, Janet (Granddaughter)
Robertson, Jessie Eva (3rd great-granddaughter)

Robertson, Keegan Jean (6th great-granddaughter)
Robertson, Loarn Despard (5th great-grandson)
Robertson, Maggie Ireland (3rd great-granddaughter)
Robertson, Mairi Alexandra (6th great-granddaughter)
Robertson, Margaret (Granddaughter)
Robertson, Margaret (2nd great-granddaughter)
Robertson, Margaret Elizabeth Pearce (4th great-granddaughter)
Robertson, Marion Hazel (4th great-granddaughter)
Robertson, Mary (Daughter)
Robertson, Maud (3rd great-granddaughter)
Robertson, Patrick James (3rd great-grandson)
Robertson, Peter (Grandson)
Robertson, Peter (2nd great-grandson)
Robertson, Rachael Despard (6th great-granddaughter)
Robertson, Ronald Douglas (3rd great-grandson)
Robertson, Rory Duncan (6th great-grandson)
Robertson, Rosemary Struan (5th great-granddaughter)
Robertson, Sophia (2nd great-granddaughter)
Scott, Anne Marlene (Wife of the 5th great-grandson)
Scott, June O'Carroll (Wife of the 4th great-grandson)
Simpson, George (Husband of the 3rd great-granddaughter)
Simpson, George Archibald Dundas (4th great-grandson)
Stewart, Anne (Wife of the great-grandson)
Strathdee, Jane Anne Finlayson (Wife of the 5th great-grandson)
Talbot-Smith, Laura Elizabeth (Wife of the 4th great-grandson)
Thallon, Janet (Wife of the 2nd great-grandson)
Wallace, Alfred Campbell (3rd great-grandson)
Wallace, Archibald Duncan (3rd great-grandson)
Wallace, Arthur Stanley Jowett (3rd great-grandson)
Wallace, James Robertson (3rd great-grandson)
Wallace, Maggie Ireland (3rd great-granddaughter)
Wallace, Patrick Robertson (3rd great-grandson)
Wallace, Robert (Husband of the 2nd great-granddaughter)
Wallace, Robert Lamb (3rd great-grandson)
Wallace, William John (3rd great-grandson)
Wills, Mary (Molly) (Wife of the 3rd great-grandson)
Wood, A. Thallon (4th great-grandson)
Wood, Charles (Husband of the 3rd great-granddaughter)

Facts and Figures

To conclude with here are a few statistics relative to this branch of the Robertson Clan.

1. There are 108 names in this branch.
2. There are 32 marriages recorded.
3. There are 10 generations.
4. The largest family unit is 10.
5. The most common male Christian name is James.
6. The most common female Christian name is Margaret.
7. The most recorded religious affiliation is Church of Scotland.
8. The oldest living member was Margorie Judd Aitken - 99+ years.
9. The wealthiest member was Sir William Arrol.
10. The best athlete was Ronald Robertson.

Figure 30. The author being interviewed about family history matters by students from Edinburgh University, in Old Greyfriars Kirkyard (2003).

Made in the USA
Middletown, DE
08 March 2022

62339939R00071